THE POWER OF CREDIT

STEP-BY-STEP GUIDE TO REPAIRING YOUR CREDIT SCORE

BY

FULTON J. TITUS

Atlas Press Publishing, LLC

The Power of Credit: Step-by-Step Guide to Repairing Your Credit Score

Imagine yourself holding the key to a treasure trove of knowledge, the secrets and strategies that will guide you through the maze of credit repair. With each step you take, you'll feel more confident and in control, as you journey towards a secure financial future. Despite life's obstacles like poor credit or no credit, our success is not determined by the difficulties we encounter, but by our response to them. Don't wait, seize this opportunity for a new beginning today with this indispensable guide.

By: Fulton J. Titus

Atlas Press Publishing, LLC

For information about special discounts for bulk purchases, inquiry....

Please contact

Atlas Press Publishing LLC: Www.AtlasPressLLC.com

Email: Info@AtlasPressLLC.com or AtlasPressAd@gmail.com

A Message of Love and Gratitude to My Children

To my dear children Sephora, Logan, and Savannah,

Dedicated to my three loved ones, this book is a symbol of my love, gratitude, and appreciation for your unwavering support. You've been my source of strength and inspiration, enabling me to bring this project to life. Your love has shown me the world in a new light and given me the courage to keep going. This book is a reminder of our family bond, and I hope it inspires you to chase your dreams with the same passion I did. Your futures are full of wonder and magic. I'm grateful to be your parent and can't wait to see what the future holds for each of you.

THE POWER OF CREDIT:

Step-by-Step Guide to Repairing Your Credit Score

AtlasPress
- PUBLISHING, LLC -

By

Fulton J. Titus

Acknowledgments

I would like to express my gratitude to all those who have supported me in the writing of this book. Firstly, I would like to thank my family and friends for their unwavering support and encouragement throughout the writing process. Without their support, this book would not have been possible.

I would also like to extend my thanks to the many experts in the fields of credit repair including my lawyer friend, Mr. Mikofsky who have shared their knowledge and insights with me, enriching the content of this book.

Finally, I would like to thank the readers for their interest in this book. Thank you for taking the time to pick up this book. It is my sincerest hope that the information and strategies contained within will help you regain control of your finances and set you on the path towards financial freedom. My goal in writing this book was to empower and educate, and I am grateful for the opportunity to share my knowledge with you.

Fulton J. Titus

Words cannot express how thankful I am to Atlas Press Publishing for their resolute support and dedication to bringing this book to life. Without their expertise, guidance, and commitment to excellence, this project would not have been possible. Their professionalism and attention to detail have been instrumental in making this book a reality, and I am honored to have had the opportunity to work with such a fantastic team. Even though this book is 2 years in the making, thank you, Atlas Press Publishing, for all that you have done to make this book a success.

Fulton J. Titus

Contents

INTRODUCTION

Life is full of possibilities, and credit is one of the most promising avenues to achieving your dreams. It's the key that unlocks doors of financial opportunities and enables you to live life on your own terms. From securing loans to leasing a car or renting an apartment, good credit is a prerequisite for almost every major financial transaction.

The American dream is an omnipresent concept that's been around for decades, and its relevance is as potent today as it was in 1929. The year 1929 was marked one of the most catastrophic events in American financial history, commonly known as the stock market crash of 1929. The crash occurred on October 29, 1929, and it led to a significant loss of wealth and widespread unemployment across the United States. The stock market lost 89% of its value, and it sent the country spiraling into the Great Depression.

The stock market crash of 1929 caused considerable financial distress for many Americans. In response to the crisis, the federal government implemented a series of measures to stimulate economic growth and provide financial assistance to those in need. These measures included the establishment of the Federal Reserve System, the implementation of the New Deal, and the creation of social security programs.

It was during this time of economic upheaval that the phrase "The American Dream" came into existence. Historians attribute the phrase to James Truslow Adams, who defined it in his 1931 book "The Epic of America" as "that dream of a land in which life should be better, richer and fuller for everyone, with opportunity for each according to ability or achievement."

History has shown us that the American Dream came to fruition during a time of tremendous economic turmoil in the 20th century. This period was marked by a devastating banking and credit crisis, which resulted in the collapse of 2293 banks and contributed to the onset of the Great Depression. During this time, 1/3 of deflationary rates for goods and services occurred, and many Americans were struggling to make ends meet. However, despite the challenges, the American Dream represented a beacon of hope and prosperity for millions of Americans, inspiring them to believe that with hard work and determination, anyone could achieve success and happiness, regardless of their background or social standing. The American Dream became a symbol of the enduring spirit of the American people, and it continues to inspire generations of Americans to strive for a better life.

As we fast forward to 2022, it's clear that the world has undergone a tectonic shift. Inflation is on the rise, and the economy is in a state of uncertainty for various domestic and international causes. In response to these challenges, the federal government is taking a range of measures to curb inflation and stimulate economic growth. This includes raising the fed's funds rate multiple times and adopting various economic policies to bolster economic activity.

As a result of these measures, mortgage rates and other financial vehicles are on the rise. This has caused a significant reduction in activities for mortgages, refinancing, and other financial investments for businesses that rely on credit. In addition, the stock market continues to be on the decline. However, amidst this financial maelstrom, there remains one constant - the importance of good credit. So, in these uncertain times, it's more important than ever to prioritize building and maintaining good credit. By doing so, you can weather the storm of economic uncertainty and position yourself for success in the long run.

Credit is a truly remarkable thing that's full of possibilities. Unlike other areas of our financial lives, credit is not set in stone. It's a dynamic force that can be improved with effort and persistence. Whether you're just starting out or rebuilding your credit after a setback, the potential is limitless. With hard work and determination, you can achieve the credit score of your dreams and unlock a world of economic potential. So, don't be discouraged, instead be inspired by the infinite potential that credit can offer.

For instance, having good credit can help you secure a mortgage for your dream home, buy a new car, start a business, or travel the world. It can help you achieve your monetary objectives and realize your dreams of financial independence. The options are endless, and the sky's the limit when it comes to what you can achieve with good credit.

Some people are lucky enough to build good credit in a matter of days, while others may take months or even years to attain the coveted status. But regardless of the time it takes, the future is always bright for those having good credit. It's the key that unlocks doors of wealth-building potential and enables you to achieve your financial objectives.

For example, with good credit, you can take advantage of low-interest rates to secure loans and investments that can help you grow your wealth. You can also negotiate better terms on your credit cards and other financial products, which can save you thousands of dollars in interest and fees.

Good credit is the key to success, whether you're an individual or a business entity. It's a powerful tool that can help you achieve your financial goals and live the life of your dreams. But to make the most of this tool, you need to have a deep understanding of the financial landscape. You need to know the rules and regulations that govern credit reporting and consumer information as it relates to the financial sector.

The journey to building good credit can be a daunting one, full of twists and turns that can leave even the most seasoned financial experts scratching their heads. However, with the right tools and knowledge, anyone can navigate this labyrinthine maze of regulations and statutes and emerge victorious on the other side. And that's what this book is all about - teaching you the resources required to have good credit for yourself, your family and friends and others.

Before we delve deeper into the world of credit repair, it's essential to have a solid understanding of the laws that govern it. While some may consider these laws daunting, we firmly believe that anyone can fix their credit with the right information and resources.

We don't want you to feel intimidated or overwhelmed by the legal landscape of credit repair. Instead, we want to empower you with the knowledge and expertise necessary to fix your credit once and for all. With a minimum understanding of the law, you can take control of your credit and improve your financial trajectory.

So, without further ado, let's dive into the law that governs credit in the United States. By understanding these laws, you can take the first step towards building good credit and realizing your financial dreams.

THE LAW OF THE LAND

The Fair Credit Reporting Act (FCRA) is a significant piece of legislation that regulates access to consumer credit report records. You can find the FCRA at 15 U.S.C. s 1681 et seq. This law aims to ensure that credit reporting agencies (CRAs) collect and report accurate, fair, and private personal information about individuals. CRAs are private companies that operate for profit by collecting and selling credit and financial information about the consumers. It's important to note that these companies are not affiliated with the U.S. government.

Under the FCRA, there are three major CRAs in the U.S. - Experian, TransUnion, and Equifax. But it's not just these big players that are subject to the law. Private investigators, detective agencies, collection agencies, and college placement offices are also considered to be CRAs under the FCRA.

One of the primary tasks of CRAs is to compile what are known as "consumer reports." These reports can include any written or oral communication by a CRA that provides information about a consumer's creditworthiness, credit standing, credit limits, character insights, general reputation, personal characteristics, or way of living and so on.... Fundamentally, these reports are a detailed summary of your credit history and financial behavior, and they can have a significant impact on your ability to secure loans, credit cards, or even a job.

In regards to accessing information contained in a consumer report, federal, state, and municipal law enforcement agencies must navigate a complex legal environment that can be difficult to understand. While these agencies can obtain basic identifying information about an individual - such as their name, address, and employment history. Through a credit reporting agency (CRA), accessing more detailed information requires a court order or subpoena.

This process can be time-consuming and challenging, and it's indispensable to have a firm grasp of the lawful requirements involved. For example, law enforcement agencies must demonstrate that the information they seek is relevant and necessary to an ongoing investigation. They must also ensure that the information they obtain is used only for lawful purposes and is not disclosed to unauthorized parties.

With respect to protecting the American public from the information collected by consumer report agencies (CRA), such as credit bureaus, medical information companies, and tenant screening services, Title VI of the Consumer Credit Protection Act plays a critical role. Under this act, the information contained in a consumer report cannot be provided to anyone who does not have a specified purpose, ensuring that individuals' personal data is kept safe and secure.

Moreover, companies that provide information to consumer report agencies have specific legal obligations under the act, including a duty to investigate disputed information in a timely manner. This ensures that inaccuracies or errors in consumer reports are corrected quickly, helping to protect consumers from unfair or damaging practices.

For users of consumer report information for credit, insurance, or employment purposes, the act requires that they notify the consumer when an adverse action is taken based on information contained in the report. This provides individuals with the opportunity to review and dispute the accuracy of the information contained in their report, helping to ensure that they are treated fairly and equitably.

The Fair and Accurate Credit Transaction Act (FACTA) added many provisions to this act, primarily relating to record accuracy and identity theft. These additions were crucial in ensuring that consumers are protected from identity theft and fraudulent practices, helping to safeguard their financial well-being.

Furthermore, the Dodd-Frank Act transferred most of the rulemaking responsibilities added by FACTA and the Credit CARD Act to the Consumer Financial Protection Bureau. However, the commission retains all of its enforcement authority as mandated by Congress, ensuring that consumer protections remain strong and effective.

In conclusion, understanding the laws and regulations surrounding credit reporting agencies and consumer reports is critical to protecting your personal and financial information, and ensuring that your credit score is accurate and reflects your financial reliability. Only by understanding the law, you can take the necessary steps to build or rebuild your credit, and achieve your financial initiatives. With the right knowledge and resources, you can navigate the nuances of credit reporting with confidence and take control of your credit score. Below is a brief overview of the 3 major credit reporting agencies:

Experian is an entity renowned for its expertise in the realm of credit reporting, serving a diverse clientele that encompasses individuals, small businesses, and large corporations alike. Established in 1996, it boasts its headquarters in the bustling city of Dublin, Ireland. With a range of financial services at its disposal, Experian empowers its clients to make informed decisions concerning credit and lending.

Through credit reporting and score analysis, identity theft protection, and additional financial services, Experian equips individuals and businesses with the tools they need to make smart choices. Boasting an impressive annual revenue of $5.2 billion USD, the company solidifies its position as one of the largest credit reporting agencies in the world.

Experian operates in over 40 countries and boasts a vast network of partnerships and alliances with leading financial institutions, enabling the company to provide its services to a global audience. With its wealth of resources and commitment to excellence, Experian is poised to continue its legacy of empowering clients with the information and tools they need to succeed.

TransUnion - Founded in 1968 and headquartered in Chicago, Illinois, TransUnion stands tall as one of the three major credit reporting agencies in the United States, flanking Experian and Equifax. Its services extend far beyond the borders of the US, catering to individuals, businesses, and government organizations in over 33 countries worldwide, including Canada and India.

With a wide range of credit reporting products, such as credit reports, credit scores, identity theft protection, and credit monitoring, TransUnion offers valuable insights and information to help individuals make informed financial decisions. On the business side, TransUnion provides risk management services, ensuring that organizations have the necessary information to make informed decisions about lending and other transactions.

Boasting an estimated revenue of $2 billion USD in 2022, TransUnion continues to dominate the credit reporting industry, offering unparalleled services and support to its global clientele.

Equifax - With a rich and storied history dating back to 1899, Equifax stands tall as one of the preeminent credit reporting agencies in the United States, and beyond. From its headquarters in Atlanta, Georgia, the company extends its reach to offer a comprehensive suite of services to consumers, businesses, and government organizations across the globe.

Equifax's offerings are diverse, spanning credit reporting and risk management, identity theft protection, fraud detection, marketing and data management services, and more. The company's credit reports and scores are renowned for their accuracy, providing critical insight and analysis to help individuals, businesses, and organizations make informed decisions about credit and lending.

With an annual revenue of approximately $2.4 billion in 2020, Equifax stands as a testament to the power and versatility of its services, providing essential support to customers in the United States and around the world. Whether you're an individual seeking to better understand your credit history, or a business looking to manage risk, Equifax is the go-to resource for unparalleled credit reporting and risk management services.

Your Rights Under the Fair Credit Reporting Act: A Summary

The federal Fair Credit Reporting Act (FCRA) promotes the accuracy, fairness, and privacy of information in the files of consumer reporting agencies. There are many types of consumer reporting agencies, including credit bureaus and specialty agencies (such as agencies that sell information about check writing histories, medical records, and rental history records). Here is a summary of your major rights under FCRA to consumer reporting agencies that operate on a nationwide basis. For more information, go to www.consumerfinance.gov/learnmore or write to: Consumer Financial Protection Bureau, 1700 G Street N.W., Washington, DC 20552.

- **You have the right to be told if information in your file has been used against you.** Anyone who uses a credit report or any other type of consumer report to deny your application for credit, insurance, or employment – or to take another adverse action against you – must tell you about it, and must give you the name, address, and phone number of the agency that provided the information.
- **You have the right to know what is in your file.** You may request and obtain all the information about you in the files of a consumer reporting agency (your "file disclosure"). You will be required to provide proper identification, which may include your Social Security number. In many cases, the disclosure will be free. You are entitled to a free file disclosure if:
    - o A person has taken adverse action against you because of the information written in your credit report.

- o You are the victim of identity theft and place a fraud alert in your file.
- o Your file contains inaccurate information as a result of fraud.
- o You are on public assistance[1].
- o You are unemployed but expect to apply for employment within 60 days.

In addition, all consumers are entitled to one free disclosure every 12 months upon request from each nationwide credit bureau and specialty consumer reporting agencies. See www.consumerfinance.gov/learnmore for additional information.

- **You have the right to ask for a credit score.** Credit scores are numerical summaries of your credit-worthiness based on information from credit bureaus. You may request a credit score from consumer reporting agencies that create scores or distribute scores used in residential real property loans, but you will have to pay for it. In some mortgage transactions, you will receive credit score information for free from the mortgage lender.
- **You have the right to dispute incomplete or inaccurate information.** If you identify information in your file that is incomplete or inaccurate, you can report it to the consumer reporting agency, the agency must investigate unless your

[1] Public assistance, also known as welfare, is a government-funded program designed to help individuals and families in need. In the United States, public assistance is provided through various programs such as Temporary Assistance for Needy Families (TANF), Supplemental Nutrition Assistance Program (SNAP), Medicaid, and others. These programs provide financial support and other forms of assistance to eligible individuals and families who are struggling to meet their basic needs due to low income, unemployment, disability, or other reasons. The goal of public assistance is to provide a safety net for those in need, so they can meet their basic needs and work towards achieving self-sufficiency.

dispute is frivolous. See www.consumerfinance.gov/learnmore for an explanation of dispute procedures.

- **Consumer reporting agencies must correct or delete inaccurate, incomplete, or unverifiable information.** Inaccurate, incomplete, or unverifiable information must be removed or corrected by reporting agencies, usually within 30 days. However, a consumer reporting agency may continue to report information it has verified as accurate.
- **Consumer reporting agencies may not report outdated negative information.** In most cases, a consumer reporting agency may not report negative information that is more than seven years old, or bankruptcies that are more than 10 years old.
- **Access to your file is limited.** A consumer reporting agency may provide information about you only to people with a valid need – usually to consider an application with a creditor, insurer, employer, landlord, or other business. The FCRA specifies those with a valid need for access.
- **You must give your consent for reports to be provided to employers.** A consumer reporting agency may not give out information about you to your employer, or a potential employer, without your written consent given to the employer. Written consent generally is not required in the trucking industry. For more information, go to www.consumerfinance.gov/learnmore.
- **You may limit "prescreened" offers of credit and insurance you get based on information in your credit report.** Unsolicited "prescreened" offers for credit and insurance must include a toll-free phone number you can call if you choose to remove your name and address from the lists these offers are based on. You may opt out with the nationwide credit bureaus at 1-888-5-OPTOUT (1-888-567-8688).

- **The right to obtain a SECURITY FREEZE[2].** You have a right to place a "security freeze" on your credit report, which will prohibit a consumer reporting agency from releasing information written in your credit report without your express authorization. The security freeze is designed to prevent credit, loans, and services from being approved in your name without your consent. However, you should be aware that using a security freeze to take control over who gets access to the personal and financial information in your credit report may delay, interfere with, or prohibit the timely approval of any subsequent request or application you make regarding a new loan, credit, mortgage, or any other account involving the extension of credit.

- **You have a right to place a security fraud alert.** As an alternative to a security freeze, you have the right to place an initial or extended fraud alert on your credit file at no cost. An initial fraud alert is a 1-year alert that is placed on a consumer's credit file. Upon seeing a fraud alert display on a consumer's credit file, a business is required to take steps to verify the consumer's identity before extending new credit. If you are a victim of identity theft, you are entitled to an extended fraud alert, which is a fraud alert lasting 7 years.

- **Consumers have a right to seek damages.** You may file a lawsuit against those who violate your rights. If a consumer reporting agency, or, in some cases, a user of consumer reports or a furnisher of information to a consumer reporting agency violates the FCRA, you may be able to sue in state or federal court.

---

[2] A security freeze does not apply to a person or entity, or its affiliates, or collection agencies acting on behalf of the person or entity, with which you have an existing account that requests information in your credit report for the purposes of reviewing or collecting the account. Reviewing the account includes activities related to account maintenance, monitoring, credit line increase, and account upgrades and enhancements.

- **Military personnel rights- Identity theft victims and active duty military members have additional rights.** Identity theft victims and active duty military personnel have additional rights under the Fair Credit Reporting Act (FCRA). For example, identity theft victims can place fraud alerts or security freezes on their credit reports to prevent new accounts from being opened in their name without their permission. Active duty military personnel can place active duty alerts on their credit reports to reduce the risk of identity theft while they are serving. Additionally, both groups have the right to free credit reports from each of the three major credit reporting agencies once a year. These additional rights aim to protect individuals who may be at a higher risk of identity theft or fraudulent activity. For more information, visit www.consumerfinance.gov/learnmore.

- **Additional rights/State laws.** Each state has the ability to enforce the regulations set forth by the Fair Credit Reporting Act (FCRA), and as such, many states have developed their own consumer reporting laws. This means that depending on where you live, you may have additional rights beyond those provided by the FCRA. For instance, in California, the Consumer Credit Reporting Agencies Act provides consumers with additional rights, such as the ability to request a copy of their credit report free of charge once per year.

- **Additional resources:**

1- To learn more about your state's consumer reporting laws, you can contact your state or local consumer protection agency or your state's Attorney General. They can provide you with information about your specific rights under state law and help you navigate any issues you may be facing.

2- If you're looking for information about your federal rights under the FCRA, you can contact the Consumer Financial Protection Bureau (CFPB). The CFPB is a government agency that is responsible for enforcing federal consumer financial laws, including the FCRA. They can provide you with information about your rights under the FCRA, as well as help you understand how to exercise those rights:

TYPE OF BUSINESS:	CONTACT:
1.a. Banks, savings associations, and credit unions with total assets of over $10 billion and their affiliates b. Such affiliates that are not banks, savings associations, or credit unions also should list, in addition to the CFPB:	a. Consumer Financial Protection Bureau 1700 G Street, N.W. Washington, DC 20552 b. Federal Trade Commission Consumer Response Center 600 Pennsylvania Avenue, N.W. Washington, DC 20580 (877) 382-4357
2. To the extent not included in item 1 above: a. National banks, federal savings associations, and federal branches and federal agencies of foreign banks b. State member banks, branches and agencies of foreign banks (other than federal branches, federal agencies, and Insured State Branches of Foreign Banks), commercial lending companies owned or controlled by foreign banks, and organizations operating under section 25 or 25A of the Federal Reserve Act. c. Nonmember Insured Banks, Insured State Branches of Foreign Banks, and insured state savings associations d. Federal Credit Unions	a. Office of the Comptroller of the Currency Customer Assistance Group 1301 McKinney Street, Suite 3450 Houston, TX 77010-9050 b. Federal Reserve Consumer Help Center P.O. Box 1200 Minneapolis, MN 55480 c. FDIC Consumer Response Center 1100 Walnut Street, Box #11 Kansas City, MO 64106 d. National Credit Union Administration Office of Consumer Financial Protection (OCFP) Division of Consumer Compliance Policy and Outreach 1775 Duke Street Alexandria, VA 22314
3. Air carriers	Asst. General Counsel for Aviation Enforcement & Proceedings Aviation Consumer Protection Division Department of Transportation 1200 New Jersey Avenue, S.E. Washington, DC 20590
4. Creditors Subject to the Surface Transportation Board	Office of Proceedings, Surface Transportation Board Department of Transportation 395 E Street, S.W. Washington, DC 20423
5. Creditors Subject to the Packers and Stockyards Act, 1921	Nearest Packers and Stockyards Administration area supervisor
6. Small Business Investment Companies	Associate Deputy Administrator for Capital Access United States Small Business Administration 409 Third Street, S.W., Suite 8200 Washington, DC 20416
7. Brokers and Dealers	Securities and Exchange Commission 100 F Street, N.E. Washington, DC 20549
8. Federal Land Banks, Federal Land Bank Associations, Federal Intermediate Credit Banks, and Production Credit Associations	Farm Credit Administration 1501 Farm Credit Drive McLean, VA 22102-5090
9. Retailers, Finance Companies, and All Other Creditors Not Listed Above	Federal Trade Commission Consumer Response Center 600 Pennsylvania Avenue, N.W. Washington, DC 20580 (877) 382-4357

CREDIT SCORE CALCULATION

Simply put, a credit score is a 3-digit number that shows important information about your financial history. The credit score's main purpose is to help lenders decide whether to grant you credit or not. It also helps employers to evaluate if a potential employee is financially responsible and so on.... Based on what I just outlined, it is safe to say that a credit score is more than just a 3 digit number. The credit score is without a doubt, the most important factor in extending or increasing credits to the consumers in the US.

The credit score associated with you was derived based on data collected by Credit Reporting Agencies (CRA). The CRA makes money by selling your information to businesses who want to see if you are creditworthy based on your overall credit score. The data was reported by your lenders to CRA. The three big CRAs are Equifax, Experian and TransUnion. Each CRA uses a different proprietary formula to the data in your credit reports to produce a score. A credit is a number typically in the range of 300 to 850 that rates credit trustworthiness by the 3 major credit bureaus. The higher the number, the better the consumer reputation to potential lenders. As a result, a credit score plays a major role in a lender's decision to offer credit.

Your credit score is important because it determines whether you will be approved for a loan and what interest rate you will pay. Prospective employers may also check to see whether you're a reliable person. In addition, service providers and utility companies may check your credit to decide whether you have to make a deposit. The credit score model was created by the Fair Isaac Corp (FICO) and is used by financial institutions throughout the US. While there are other credit scoring models, the FICO score is by far the most commonly used in the industry.

What is a FICO Score

The Fair Isaac Corporation (FICO) score was introduced to the credit industry in 1989 with the aim of providing a standard for evaluating creditworthiness that was fair to both lenders and consumers. Prior to the FICO score, there were many different credit scores, all calculated differently, leading to a biased and unobjective system. The FICO score was created to provide a consistent and fact-based evaluation of credit dependability.

The FICO score is a three-digit number based on the information in your credit reports. It is important to lenders as it helps them determine how likely you are to repay a loan. For example, if you have a high FICO score, it is more likely that you will be approved for a mortgage or auto loan, and you may receive a lower interest rate. If you have a low FICO score, you may not be approved for a loan, or you may receive a higher interest rate.

Your FICO score is determined by several factors, including your payment history, credit utilization, length of credit history, and types of credit accounts. For instance, paying your bills on time and using credit responsibly can increase your FICO score, while missing payments and maxing out credit cards can lower it.

In short, your FICO score reflects your financial strength and likelihood of repaying a loan. It's a good idea to keep track of your score and work to improve it if necessary, as it can impact your ability to obtain credit and the terms of that credit.

UNDERSTANDING YOUR FICO SCORE

Credit scores, such as the widely used FICO score, play a critical role in determining your financial health. Banks, credit card companies, and other lenders use credit scores to determine the likelihood of a borrower repaying their debts. The higher the credit score, the more likely the borrower is to be approved for loans or credit cards with better terms and lower interest rates.

However, it's crucial to note that there are other types of credit scores in addition to FICO. VantageScore, for example, is another popular credit scoring model that ranges from 300 to 850, similar to FICO. Some lenders may also use industry-specific credit scoring models, such as the FICO Auto Score for car loans or the FICO Bankcard Score for credit card applications.

Credit scores are not set in stone and can change over time as credit behavior changes. Factors that can affect credit scores include payment history, amounts owed, length of credit history, new credit applications, and credit mix.

It's also worth mentioning that different credit reporting agencies may use different scoring models, which can lead to variations in scores. For example, Experian may use the VantageScore model, while Equifax and TransUnion may use the FICO model.

- Please keep in mind that lenders use different scores depending on the products
- There are different credit scoring models
- Information that makes up the credit score come from different CRA

As different lenders use different credit score models, an individual may qualify for lower rates with one lender and higher with another one. Therefore, it is advisable to shop around and compare rates from multiple lenders before applying for a loan. However, it is important to limit hard inquiries[3] on your credit report as they can negatively impact your credit score.

FICO SCORE VS CREDIT SCORE

FICO scores are not a one-size-fits-all type of credit score. There are different types of FICO scores that are used by lenders to evaluate one's financial reliability.

The most commonly used FICO score is FICO 8, which was introduced in 2009. FICO 8 uses information from credit reports to generate a three-digit score ranging from 300 to 850. This score is used by many lenders to determine financial stability, and it takes into account a person's payment history, credit utilization, length of credit history, types of credit used, and recent credit inquiries.

FICO 9 is a newer version of the FICO score that was introduced in 2014. It includes some changes in how medical debt is considered and also disregards paid collection accounts. This means that if you are having trouble paying your medical debts,

[3] A hard inquiry, also known as a hard pull, is a type of credit check that is performed when a lender or creditor requests to view your credit report. This happens when you apply for a loan, credit card, or other type of credit. Hard inquiries can have a negative impact on your credit score because they indicate that you are seeking new credit and can be seen as a sign of increased risk to lenders. Each hard inquiry can lower your credit score by a few points, and multiple hard inquiries within a short period of time can have a larger impact. It's important to be mindful of the number of hard inquiries on your credit report and to only apply for credit when necessary.

In this book, we provide an in-depth discussion of hard inquiries and how they can impact your credit score. It's important to understand how these inquiries work, especially if you're planning on shopping around for loans or credit cards. By limiting the number of hard inquiries on your credit report, you can improve your chances of qualifying for lower rates and better terms.

the collection agencies may not be able to help you as much. This can lead to higher scores for some consumers.

FICO 10 and FICO 10T are even newer versions of the FICO score, which were introduced in 2020. These scores are designed to be more predictive of a borrower's future credit risk. FICO 10T uses trended credit data, which means that it takes into account a borrower's credit behavior over time.

Another type of FICO score is the UltraFICO score. It is designed to help people who have little or no credit history to establish credit or rebuild their credit score. UltraFICO uses information from checking, savings, and money market accounts to calculate credit scores. This score takes into account how frequently an account is used, how much money is in the account, and for how long the account has been opened.

Understanding the different FICO score models can be useful for consumers who are trying to improve their credit. A popular other credit score is called VantageScore which we also covered in this book. Depending on the lender and the type of credit being applied for, different score models may be used to evaluate credit standing. Monitoring your credit report and being aware of the credit score models being used are crucial to understanding your credit score. By doing so, you can take advantage of this information and make informed decisions to benefit yourself and your family.

FICO vs. VantageScore

The VantageScore model is another credit score that was introduced in 2006 and jointly developed by the three major credit bureaus. While FICO is still more widely used and well-known by consumers and lenders in the USA, VantageScore is gaining popularity in the industry. It is estimated that FICO is used in at least 90% of lending decisions, and it is the only tool approved by government-sponsored enterprises such as Fannie Mae and Freddie Mac for evaluating credit risk, particularly for home mortgages.

However, in October 2022, the Federal Housing Finance Agency required the use of FICO 10T and VantageScore 4.0 for mortgage loans sold to Fannie and Freddie. Although implementation of these two newer scoring models will take "a multiyear effort" to be fully adopted by the mortgage industry, the benefits are expected to be significant, especially for minority home buyers.

WHAT IS A GOOD FICO SCORE?

Generally, scores from 690 to 719 are considered good credit. The FICO company itself defines a good score range between 670-739. Different lenders or credit card issuers can decide what score is needed to qualify based on their adopted criteria.

Having a FICO score that falls within the good or excellent range can provide you with a wider range of choices and access to lower interest rates. This can also give you more options when it comes to lending programs, which can be beneficial in helping you achieve your economic aspirations. By maintaining a good FICO score, you can take advantage of these benefits and make well-informed choices that will benefit you and your family.

Below are the different variables of your credit file that weigh heavily in a great credit score:

- **Credit History /Trade lines** - A long credit history conveys confidence in the overall scoring model. Since credit scores are based on experience over time, your score improves over time. The longer your credit history the better it is for the lender to make a decision on your application.
- **Credit card utilization** – A good rule of thumb according to the expert is under 30%. That means if you have a $1,000 credit limit, you should only be using less than $300 of the credit.
- **Derogatory marks**[4] – These derogatory marks really hurt your score. These marks can be collection accounts, charge-offs, student loans, bankruptcies and so on...
- **Credit age** – The longer you are able to maintain credit, the more appealing you are to the potential creditors. The reason is that the creditors are able to review and verify past credit performances.
- **Total accounts** – The important thing is to make sure that you use your credit responsibly. Too many accounts can hurt your credit score.
- **Hard inquiries** – A hard inquiry or a "hard pull" occurs when you apply for a new credit line such as a credit card or loan. It

[4] Derogatory marks are negative items that are reported to a credit bureau and appear on a person's credit report. These marks can include items such as late payments, collections, foreclosures, repossessions, and bankruptcies. Derogatory marks can have a significant impact on a person's credit score and can make it more difficult for them to obtain credit or loans in the future. It's important for individuals to review their credit report regularly to monitor for any derogatory marks and to take steps to correct any inaccuracies or dispute any errors that may appear on their credit report.

means that you have authorized a creditor to review your credit report for the purpose of extending credit to you.

Your credit score can make or break you because it depicts your credit strength at the time. The right credit score can impact your life in a meaningful way. Simply put, a credit score represents your financial strength. The credit card companies, the mortgage companies, auto loan companies and other creditors use your credit score to determine your credit risk. Obviously, the higher the credit score, the less risk is associated with your application and vice versa. So it makes sense for you as a consumer to have as high a credit score as possible. The credit score in a nutshell tells a picture about you. It tells the bank or the creditor about your ability to repay the debt; it tells them about your past credit performance as an indication of your future performance; it tells them about current debt and so on...

The Fair Isaac Company, which created the FICO score, doesn't publicly disclose the precise formula used to calculate a person's credit score due to its proprietary nature. However, what is known is that the calculation is composed of five major categories, which are fundamental to assessing a person's financial stability. These categories are payment history, amounts owed, credit history length, types of accounts, and recent credit activity.

1- **Payment history:** This category accounts for 35% of your FICO score and reflects whether you have made payments on time in the past. Late payments, collections, and bankruptcies can all lower your score.

2- **Amounts owed:** This category makes up 30% of your FICO score and considers the amount of debt you currently owe. High levels of debt relative to your credit limits can lower your score.

3- **Credit history length:** This category contributes to 15% of your FICO score and takes into account how long you've been using credit. A long credit history is typically better for your score than a short one.

4- **Types of accounts:** This category makes up 10% of your FICO score and looks at the different types of credit accounts you have, such as credit cards, loans, and mortgages.

5- **Recent credit activity:** This category accounts for the remaining 10% of your FICO score and considers how recently you've opened new credit accounts or had credit inquiries. Applying for multiple new credit accounts in a short period of time can negatively impact your score.

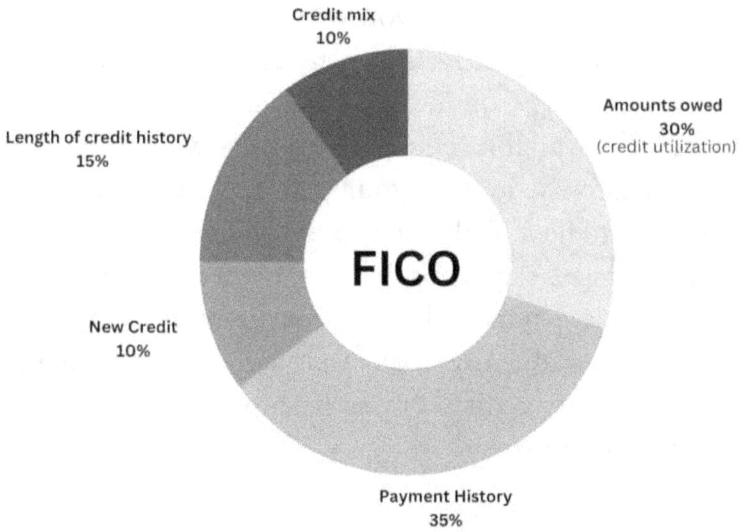

FICO Credit Scoring Factors

PAYMENT HISTORY - 35%

One's payment history accounts for 35% of your overall score. This represents whether or not a person makes timely payments or how often you miss payments. Any payments made over 30 days late will be reported by your lender and in essence lower your credit score. Payment history also shows how many accounts that show late payments and whether or not you've brought the accounts current. Your score will be highest in proportion to how much on-time payments you have successfully made on the account. Please keep in mind that every time you miss a payment, that will negatively impact your overall score.

HOW MUCH MONEY YOU OWE - 30%

This portion makes up to 30% of your overall score. This measures the entire amount you owe including the number and types of accounts you have. Also, the credit modeling model will calculate the amount of money owed compared to how much credit you have available. High balances known as high utilization rate will negatively impact your score. That's why it is very important not to have high balances or maxed-out the credit cards or the loan. Please keep in mind even though you pay on-time, new loans with little payment history may temporarily lower your credit score. Consequently, loans that are closer to being paid off may increase your credit score as it shows that you successfully meet your debt obligations.

THE LENGTH OF YOUR CREDIT HISTORY - 15%

As any other factor of your credit score, this is also important as this accounts for roughly 15% of your score. This is basically simple. The longer your credit history of making on-time payments and managing the account well, the better impact it will have on your overall credit score. Most credit scoring models will look at the average age of your credit to determine the strength of the credit. This is why it is utmost important to consider keeping your accounts open and active. The job of the lender will be incomplete if they are unable to verify credit history. As a result, your application will not be as robust as someone with a longer credit history.

TYPES OF ACCOUNTS YOU HAVE- 10%

This makes up about 10% of your overall score. Having a mixture of different accounts including installment loans, home loans, credit cards and charge cards may help improve your score. This is important because the creditor is able to measure how well you manage different types of debts.

RECENT CREDIT ACTIVITY - 10%

This makes up about 10% of your overall credit score. If you recently opened a lot of accounts or applied for a number of open accounts, it may suggest a potential financial risk for the creditors. This inevitably lowers your credit score and ultimately decreases your chances of getting approved. All credit scoring models are designed to recognize recent loan activities which may or may not represent added financial risk for the creditors.

Now that you have understood how your credit score is tabulated based on five key principles, let's dive into how you can improve your credit. The most effective way to potentially boost your credit score is to use credit responsibly by making on-time payments and keeping your credit utilization rate low. A good mix of credit accounts, such as a combination of credit cards and loans, can also benefit your score.

By demonstrating positive credit habits over time, you can show lenders that you are a responsible borrower which will increase your chances of being approved for credit at a competitive rate. Keep in mind that consumers with high credit scores typically receive the lowest interest rates on overall costs of credit. This makes having a good credit score a win-win situation for both the consumer and the lender.

TIPS AND TRICKS TO BUILD OR REBUILD CREDIT QUICKLY

People with low credit scores may have a harder time accessing much needed credit and are often charged higher interest rates on credit cards, loans and mortgages. Hopefully you understand by now that poor credit is very expensive in America. While there is no magic formula to building credit quickly, there are however a few steps you can take to ensure that poor credit will be in your rear view mirror. The most important thing to understand is that rebuilding credit is possible but it will happen over time. One has to be patient and definitely has to be responsible. If your ultimate destination is a high credit score by building or rebuilding your credit, I encourage you to follow these steps:

- **Pay off your debt if you can** – making payments on time to your lenders is the biggest contributing factor to achieving a high credit score.
- **Get a secured credit card** – Secured credit card is a way that extends credit to you in exchange for a refundable security deposit. A secured credit card offers a lot of great benefits. It helps everyone that has either poor credit or someone trying

to rebuild their credit. You can go to your local bank or check on CreditKarma.com for various creditors that offer this product.

- **Get a credit builder loan** - This is great for people with no credit history or short credit history. No credit needed to qualify but may require a certain income threshold.

- **Increase credit limit-**If you have a credit card with a creditor, I recommend you ask for a credit limit increase to improve your utilization rate. However, you have to be careful to use your new credit increase responsibly.

- **Open a PRBC account to get a credit score** - PRBC stands for "Pay Rent, Build Credit, Inc. The company was established to report all recurring bills and loan payments including utilities and Rent. To add a PRBC score and report, you would need to become a member to report your rent, your electric bill, your cable bill or even online services. When you pay your bills on time, PRBC would report your good habits and will raise your credit score. You can open a PRBC account at: Www. Prbc.com. Make sure to add all your good standing accounts.

- **Add Experian boost** – You can instantly increase your credit score by using Experian Credit boost by adding your utilities and rent payments. Consumers can add rent, streaming, cell phone and utility payments in their Experian credit report to build or rebuild credit. This is a great method but unfortunately only Experian credit scores will be affected.

- **Become an authorized user**- This is also called a "piggybacker" or the 'backdoor" method which is a person authorized to use someone else's credit card whereas the primary cardholder is solely responsible for all the debts on the card – regardless of who makes the charges. Pickybacker or backdoor refers to the way in which the entire credit history of the primary account holder gets transferred to the authorized user. The entire credit card history – good or bad- is included in the authorized user profile. So it's a good idea to make sure you're becoming an authorized user on a primary account holder with a positive credit profile. Otherwise, this could backfire and result in a worse credit score than before you became an authorized user. Keep in mind that whoever you use should have good credit management skills. Don't use someone that's constantly making late payments and has a high credit utilization rate as both the positives and negatives will be reported. Make sure that the credit card company reports on authorized users. According to the Nerd wallet, these cards are reported.

Issuer	Does the Issuer report authorized user activity to the credit bureaus?
American Express	Yes, if the account isn't delinquent and the authorized user is at least 18
Bank of America	Yes
Barclays	Yes, if the authorized user is at least 16
Discover	Yes, Discover requires its if the authorized user is at least 16
Capital One	Yes
Citi	Yes
Chase	Yes
U.S. Bank	Yes, unless the primary account is delinquent
Wells Fargo	Yes, if the authorized user is at least 18

TIPS AND TRICKS TO RAISE YOUR CREDIT SCORE 750+ POINT

An excellent credit score is the cornerstone of financial stability and prosperity, as it unlocks doors to a variety of opportunities such as loans or credit cards with favorable terms, rental agreements, and employment. However, if your credit score is below 750, do not be disheartened, because with the right strategies and knowledge, you can improve your credit score and achieve a 750+ score. In this guide, we will share some insightful tips and tricks that will help you elevate your credit score to new heights, allowing you to achieve your financial objectives. So, let's dive in and begin building a better credit future!

- Paying your bills on time every month has the greatest impact on your score. An authentic way to make sure you pay your bills on time and not worry about a late payment is to set up Automatic payments. If life happens and you miss a payment, get current and stay current.
- Credit scoring models look at different factors but they mainly look at how close you are to being “maxed out” of your credit limit. Keeping your balances low and under 30% of your credit limit should be the goal. That will serve you best for maximum credit score.
- Call all your credit card companies and ask for an increase to your limit which will lower your utilization rate.
- You can apply for new credit cards which will also lower your utilization rate based on the new credit line amount. You can utilize creditKarma.com for recommendations on credit cards you’re pre-approved based on your credit score. * You can also go to creditcards.com and apply for cards for bad credit

- Be mindful that a close account can hurt your score. Closing a card and putting most or all of your credit card balances in just one card may hurt your score as it will produce a high percentage of your total credit limit. Closing and opening different account balances can ultimately hurt your credit score. So be careful.

- Limit the amount of new and closed accounts. When you open a new account you risk ruining the other categories that calculate your credit score which is length of credit history and inquiries.

- Only apply for credit you need. The credit score model analyzes recent credit activity to predict your need for credit. When someone applies for a lot of credit in a short period of time, it may indicate that your money situation has changed for the worse. In other words, the bank will not lend you money if they think that you are completely under water.

- Become an authorized user on a great account. Be careful with becoming an authorized user as the wrong authorized user can hurt your credit score. The ideal situation is for you to be an authorized user on someone's account who is responsible, pays on-time and has low credit utilization preferably under 30%.

- Consider applying for a Home Equity Line of Credit called a HELOC loan. A HELOC is a loan in which the lender agrees to lend a maximum amount with an agreed period (called a term), where your house will be used as provided that you have enough equity in the home. You can use a HELOC loan to pay your credit cards down to 10%. There are dual benefits to doing that: 1st your utilization will go down which will raise your credit score and 2nd the interest amount on your HELOC loan is tax deductible whereas no interest on credit cards. You can go on lendingtree.com and shop for the best HELOC loan.

☞ *Credit tips:* FICO doesn't consider all account types as being equal. Revolving balances like credit and retail cards tend to carry more weight than installment debt like mortgage, auto and student loans. As a result, credit cards are the most important type of account for achieving the highest FICO score, but they can also cause more damage to your overall score than other types of credit.

☞ *Credit tips:* Do not close an unused or unwanted credit card due to the impact of the utilization ratio calculation. If you close an account, your utilization rate will increase which will cause your overall score to decrease. So be cognizant that closing a credit card is not a good idea.

☞ *Credit tips:* You should consider making payments to your creditors more than one a month. If you charge a major expense like a new Flat Screen TV, your FICO score might be impacted negatively. Let me explain. The reason is that your FICO score is calculated as a snapshot in time, so if that happens to be right after your large purchase, your utilization ratio will reflect the transaction and as an outcome your utilization rate will be high. Hence, there is a greater probability that your score will go down.

SOME PERKS FOR HAVING GOOD CREDIT SCORE

Having a good credit score is more than just a number, it is an important tool for achieving financial stability and prosperity. One of the most significant benefits of having a good credit score is that consumers are more likely to meet lending approval guidelines and borrow money when they need it most. Moreover, it is a well-known fact that the best credit cards require at least a good credit score. With a good credit score, you can take full advantage of the best introductory offers, reward incentives on new credit cards and negotiate the best terms. In addition to the obvious benefits, consumers with better credit scores can receive special invitations to exclusive events, free access to online streaming services, and many other perks. Therefore, it is necessary to maintain a good credit score to take advantage of these opportunities for growth and enjoy the best things in life. Below are 13 fundamental reasons why having good credit is so important:

1. **Emergencies:** Having good credit provides access to money during unexpected events, such as medical emergencies, job loss, or home repairs. For example, if your car breaks down and you need a new one, a good credit score will make it easier to obtain an auto loan with favorable terms.
2. **Business:** Good credit can provide access to funding for starting or expanding a business. For example, a small business owner with good credit may be able to secure a business loan with a lower interest rate, which can help them to grow and expand their business.
3. **Mortgages and Home Equity Loans:** A good credit score is necessary to qualify for a mortgage or home equity loan. For example, a borrower with a credit score of 750 may be able to obtain a mortgage with a lower interest rate, which can save them thousands of dollars over the life of the loan.

4. **Unsecured Loans:** Good credit can help you qualify for unsecured loans, which do not require collateral. For example, a borrower with good credit may be able to obtain a personal loan with a lower interest rate, which can be used for a variety of purposes such as consolidating debt or financing a large purchase.
5. **Auto Loans:** Having good credit can also help you obtain better rates on auto loans. For example, a borrower with a credit score of 700 may be able to obtain an auto loan with a lower interest rate than someone with a credit score of 600.
6. **Employment:** Some employers may require good credit as a condition of employment, particularly for jobs that involve handling money or sensitive information. For example, a job applicant with a history of financial responsibility may be viewed more favorably by an employer than someone with a poor credit history.
7. **Rewards Credit Cards:** Having good credit can provide access to rewards on credit cards that offer cash back, travel rewards, or other perks. For example, a cardholder with a good credit score may be able to qualify for a credit card that offers airline miles or hotel points.
8. **Purchase Protection:** Many credit cards offer purchase protection, which can protect against fraud or other issues with purchases. For example, a cardholder may be able to dispute a fraudulent charge or receive a refund if a merchant refuses to honor a return.
9. **Travel Protection:** Some credit cards offer travel protection, such as trip cancellation insurance or rental car insurance. For example, a cardholder may be covered if their flight is canceled due to weather or if their rental car is damaged.
10. **No Deposits:** Good credit can also help you avoid security deposits on utilities or leases. For example, a renter with good

credit may be able to avoid paying a security deposit when signing a lease.

11. **Insurance:** Having good credit can help you obtain the best rates on car and homeowner's insurance. For example, a homeowner with good credit may be able to obtain a lower premium on their homeowner's insurance policy.
12. **Zero Liability:** Many credit cards offer zero liability protection, which can protect against unauthorized charges. For example, a cardholder may not be responsible for charges that were made on their card without their knowledge.
13. **Lower Interest Rates:** Perhaps the most important reason to have good credit is that it can make borrowing money cheaper. For example, a borrower with good credit may be able to obtain a loan with a lower interest rate than someone with poor credit, which can save them hundreds or even thousands of dollars over the life of the loan.

CREDIT REPAIR IN A NUTSHELL

As the famous Chinese saying goes, "a journey of a thousand miles begins with the first step." The same can be said for credit repair. It may seem overwhelming, but the key is to take that first step and stay persistent. Many people believe credit repair to be a difficult task, but it is achievable with the right mindset and determination. It is important to accept the journey and not give up, no matter what obstacles may come your way. Remember, life is what you make it and anything worthwhile requires a certain amount of energy and unyielding determination, including credit repair.

Credit repair isn't going to happen overnight, but it happens faster than you think. It is easier if you know what you're doing. My main goal for writing this book is to prevent people from getting scammed out of thousands of dollars on credit repair services that offer little and protracted time in order to make as much money from you as possible via monthly subscription fees. I'm sure you have heard about the credit repair companies that billed you every month for credit repair services. At most times, months turn into years of credit repair services and sometimes, all your issues are not solved but yet you still have to pay hefty monthly fees. I want people to know that they can take matters into their own hands. People can actually repair their credit by themselves. As shocking as it may seem, I will lay out all the secrets that credit repairs use to repair credits. Again, my main goal is to educate the public about credit repairs.

Please be careful that it's important to complete some preliminary work prior to disputing the negative items on your credit report. You don't just get up on your bed and go to work. What most people do is wake up, take a shower, get dressed, have breakfast/coffee and then go to work. Credit repair works the same way. You don't just write letters and expect that in a few weeks, all your negative items are removed. It doesn't work that way. There are certain steps that need to be done in order to have the best chance of removing adverse accounts on your credit.

To increase your chances of success, it's imperative to take the right steps when it comes to credit repair. You may have heard about the infamous 609 letters (see What is Section 609). Some credit repair companies charge exorbitant fees for the "ultimate" 609 template letters, promising that they're the perfect solution. But let me tell you, just sending out template 609 letters to the credit bureaus won't work most of the time.

The truth is, the industry knows that these expensive template letters are useless. Most of the time, nobody will even read your letters. Instead, the 609 letters are scanned by a computer and assigned a two-digit code called an E-OSCAR code. This software was created by the big credit bureaus in 1993 to streamline their reporting/dispute process. So, while the 609 letters may seem like a quick fix, they're not the best way to improve your credit.

I will outline all the steps you need in order to fix your credit once and for all. I'm happy to be your guide in your credit repair journey. I will include my email address if you want to contact me about your progress. I hope nothing but to hear good news. I want to hear about the mortgage you have now qualified for. I want to know about the car you were able to buy. I want to know about the credit cards that you applied to and got approved. All these stories are truly special to me. Again, don't give up and stay the course. To begin learning about credit repair, it's helpful to understand how the process works. One good starting point is to learn about e-Oscar.

What is e-OSCAR

In order to ensure that mistakes or errors on credit reports might be investigated in a timely manner, the e-OSCAR (Online Solution for Complete and Accurate Reporting) system was created in 1993. Owned by four credit reporting companies — Equifax, Experian, Innovis, and TransUnion — e-OSCAR gives these companies a means of investigating credit reporting disputes without ever dispatching a human employee. Sometimes the system works well and disputes are resolved quickly and definitively. However, consumer complaints are often complicated, as they involve real-world breakdowns of our credit reporting systems. Not all complaints fit well into a two digit E-OSCAR code as the correction process may require further investigation.

Contrary to popular misconceptions, Credit disputes involve a 3-step process:

1. The credit bureau receives a credit dispute letter.
2. A computer scan/ or employee reads the letter and assigns one of e-OSCAR's 29 three-digit codes to classify the type of error.
3. The computer/ employee enters this code along with basic information about the consumer and creditor. They may also enter one or two lines of explanation.

The e-OSCAR Coding system

When you dispute an error on your credit report, the credit reporting agency will process your request and input it into the e-OSCAR system. This system is designed to categorize your dispute into one of approximately 30 three-digit dispute codes, which are used to determine the nature of the issue you're facing. These codes include:

- 001 — Not his/hers.
- 002 — Belongs to another individual with the same/similar name.
- 006 — Not aware of the collection.
- 008 — Late due to change of address and never received a statement.
- 010 — Settlement or partial payments accepted.
- 012 — Claims paid the original creditor before collection status or paid before charge-off.
- 014 — Claims paid before collection status.
- 019 — Included in the bankruptcy of another person.
- 023 — Claims account closed.
- 024 — Claims account closed by consumer.
- 031 — Contract canceled or rescinded.
- 037 — Account included in bankruptcy.
- 038 — Claims active military duty.
- 039 — Insurance claim delayed.
- 040 — Account involved in litigation.
- 041 — Claims victim of natural or declared disaster.
- 100 — Claims account deferred.
- 101 — Not liable for account (i.e. account belongs to ex-spouse, business, etc)
- 102 — Account reaffirmed or not included in bankruptcy.
- 103 — Claims true identity fraud/account fraudulently opened.
- 104 — Claims account take-over, fraudulent charges made on account.
- 105 — Disputes Dates of Last Payment/Opened/ of First Delinquency/Billing/Closed.

- 106 — Disputes present/previous Account Status/Payment History Profile/Payment Rating.
- 107 — Disputes Special Comment/Compliance Condition Code/narrative remarks.
- 108 — Disputes Account Type or Terms Duration/Terms Frequency or Portfolio Type disputed.
- 109 — Dispute current balance.
- 110 — Claims company will change.
- 111 — Claims company will delete.
- 112 — Claims inaccurate information.

Furthermore, apart from selecting the appropriate dispute code, if necessary, the credit reporting agency may also provide a brief explanation of the dispute. Once this information is received by the e-OSCAR system, it generates and archives a formal dispute, and then transmits the relevant data to the other credit reporting agencies and the relevant data providers for further investigation.

Problems With e-OSCAR

While e-OSCAR does allow for the efficient processing of some credit reporting disputes, it is not without its problems. Consumer rights advocates complain that the E-OSCAR system doesn't always capture the details of a consumer's dispute. A mischaracterized complaint can drag out the time it takes to fix the error on the consumer's credit report. In addition, supporting documents are not always transferred in a consumer's complaint, meaning that information important to a dispute does not always follow that consumer's dispute through the investigation process.

A congressional report in 2007 found that e-OSCAR reports used the same two dispute codes over 90% of the time, calling into question the value of the 29 codes. That same report found that, through the e-OSCAR system, credit reporting bureaus never actually investigate disputes, instead choosing to simply repeat a consumer's complaints to data furnishers.

What is Section 609

Section 609 of the Fair Credit Reporting Act (FCRA) outlines a consumer's right to order copies of their credit report and the information that appears on it for the sole purpose of examining such information. Section 609 aims to protect your right to dispute inaccurate information on your credit report. Even though the right to dispute the information is not explicitly expressed, it is an implied right for a consumer to check and verify the information contained in the credit report. Furthermore, section 609 gives you the right for transparency with the CRA meaning that you have a right to examine the information contained in your credit file.

When you understand your rights under section 609, you can take charge of your credit file. You can then take the necessary steps to learn how to protect your credit reports. This is key to fixing your credit as the credit score is based on the information in your credit file and it is a representation of how responsible you are with your financial life and your ability or inability to pay bills on time.

Under section 609, you have the right to request from the CRA the following:

1- All of the information in your credit files.

2- The source(s) of that information.

3- Each entity that accessed your credit report within a certain time period.

4- Businesses or organizations that have made hard/soft inquiries.

Section 609 and Section 611 of the statute establish that if disputed information cannot be verified or confirmed, it must be removed from your credit report. Interestingly, Section 609 does not directly pertain to your rights to dispute information, but instead, it has become synonymous with credit dispute due to its frequent use. The actual language outlining your rights to dispute information in your credit report is contained in Section 611. Despite this, the term "609 Dispute letters[5]" is often used to refer to the process of disputing information on your credit report. However, for legal purposes, a 609 dispute letter is not technically a dispute, but rather a request for documentation from the credit bureau to substantiate the accuracy of the information in your credit report. We will explore in detail the topic of 609 dispute letters in later chapters to provide a more detailed understanding.

What to Know About Credit Disputes

In agreement with the Fair Credit Reporting Act (FCRA), the Consumer Reporting Agency (CRA) has up to 30 days plus an additional 15 days to resolve a dispute. If the error involves an account with your creditor, the credit bureau will usually reach out to investigate the item you reported. It is reported that CRA's resolve only 15% of complaints without involving the data furnisher. After you provide a response to the dispute in question, the CRA will notify you of the outcome. The error will either be validated and will be corrected, or they have determined there was

[5] The 609 provision specifically refers to section 609 of the FCRA, which outlines the process for requesting and obtaining a copy of your credit report. Over time, the 609 dispute letter has become a popular method for disputing negative or inaccurate items on a credit report, although its effectiveness is not guaranteed and there are other methods for disputing credit report information

no error and the item is reported as accurate on your updated credit report.

According to the Federal Trade Commission, at least 1 in 5 consumers has an error on one of their three credit reports and 1 in 4 of these errors have a negative impact on the consumers' overall credit scores. Most mistakes can be pinned down to creditors or other companies providing information to the credit bureaus. Some errors are intentional and some are not. Other mistakes can be attributed to human error. It is recommended that you check your credit report often and report anything that seems incorrect.

If you find there is something wrong on your credit report, you may contact both the credit reporting company and the company that provided the information to the CRA like the credit card company or the bank. You should explain the error on your credit report and ask them to update your report accordingly. You may be able to include supporting documents in support of your dispute. In a perfect world, that is all that's needed to fix the errors. Simply call the CRA or the lender and then the problem will be corrected. Unfortunately, that's not always the case. It is not that simple. You may have to revert to other means which I will show you on how to properly correct mistakes on your credit report.

CREDIT REPAIR SECRETS 101

By now, you should understand the importance of having a good credit score. It is the main tool used by creditors to evaluate your creditworthiness, and it can impact your ability to borrow money or obtain a job. However, improving your credit score requires consistent effort and patience. It is not something that can be fixed overnight, but with the right knowledge and tools, you can achieve an outstanding credit score in no time.

That's why this book was created - to teach you everything you need to know about repairing or rebuilding your credit. With the methods and strategies outlined in this book, you can learn how to take control of your credit score and make positive changes that will benefit you for years to come. Whether you are starting from scratch or trying to fix past mistakes, this book will provide you with the support and resources to achieve your goals. So, take the first step towards a better financial future and dive into the world of credit repair today!

In the US, the average credit score stands at 698 as per 2021 data. However, not everyone has a good credit score, especially if it falls below 670. A poor or low credit score can prevent you from achieving many things, such as buying a car, purchasing a home, or even obtaining a credit card. Your credit score has a significant impact on your financial future, particularly when it comes to borrowing money.

It's indispensable to know that you don't have just one credit score. Different lenders or institutions use different scoring models based on your past financial experiences. Factors like how well you've paid off credit accounts, how much credit you use, and how long you've had credit, all contribute to your credit score. Positive and negative past credit events also play a role. If you've had a bankruptcy in the past, for example, it can hurt your overall credit score. It's crucial to work on improving your credit score so that you can have more financial avenues and a better future.

If you're looking to improve your credit file to obtain better credit, you're in luck. This book provides a step-by-step approach to fixing your credit report and achieving a higher credit score. It's important to follow three critical steps in order to achieve the best possible outcome. Let's get started without delay.

STEP 1: Get a copy of your credit report:

As mandated by the Fair Credit Act, all consumer reporting companies must furnish you with a copy of your credit file upon request. Most credit reporting companies will provide this report free of charge, but some charge a small fee in accordance with the Act. According to the Fair Credit Reporting Act, the companies can’t charge more than $12 for your report. Some companies allow you to request a free report online.

The Fair Credit Report Act also mandates a free report, regardless of the credit agency's fee policy, if information in your report causes a negative decision to be made against you within a certain time frame. Without further ado, let's discuss the 1st step in your credit repair journey.

The 1st step in your journey to fix your credit is to actually obtain a copy of your credit report. You have to know what's in your actual credit report so that you can develop a strategy to fix it. As per law of the U.S., you can get a free copy of your credit report every 12 months.

You can choose to request your credit reports from each credit reporting company at different times throughout the year. There is no requirement to order all three credit reports simultaneously. A top choice for many Americans is to get their credit report from Annualcreditreport.com[6] which provides your credit reports from all 3 credit bureaus. There are three ways to request your free annual credit report: online, by phone, or through mail.

Online:

You can ask for your free annual credit report from https://www.AnnualCreditReport.com. This is the official site, authorized by the Federal government, for you to get your free reports. You can usually get access to your report immediately to process pending verification of your identity through an authentication process.

---

[6] AnnualCreditReport.com is a website that provides consumers with a free credit report from each of the three major credit bureaus - Equifax, Experian, and TransUnion - once a year. The website is authorized by federal law and is managed by the three credit bureaus in partnership with the Federal Trade Commission (FTC). The funding for the website comes from the credit bureaus themselves, as they are required by law to provide consumers with a free credit report every year.

Phone:

- Call 1 877-322-8228.
- You will request a credit report through a verification process over the phone.
- Your credit report will be mailed within 15 days.

Mail:

- Download the request form: https://www.annualcreditreport.com/manualRequestForm.action
- Print and complete the form
- Mail the completed form to:
    - Annual Credit Report Service
    - P.O. Box 105281
    - Atlanta, GA 30348-5281

Below is the contact information for all 3 credit bureaus you can decide to request your free credit report from them directly. Again, the free annual credit report will contain your credit information as reported from all 3 major credit bureaus.

Credit Reporting Agency	Address	Telephone Number	Webpage
Equifax	Equifax Disclosure Department P.O. Box 740241 Atlanta, GA 30374	(800) 685-1111	www.equifax.com/fcra
Experian	Experian 701 Experian Parkway P.O. Box 2002 Allen, TX 75013	1-888-EXPERIAN (1-888-397-3742)	www.experian.com/reportaccess
Transunion	Transunion Consumer Relations 2 Baldwin Place P.O. Box 1000 Chester, PA 19016	1-800-888-4213	www.transunion.com/myoptions

CAUTION: Getting a free credit report online from the 3 credit bureaus forces you to waive your rights to sue them in the event of a conflict. This means that in the event your only alternative is to sue them, the term of services forces you to go into arbitration[7] with them. All three major credit bureaus have arbitration agreements in their terms of use. Your rights to a jury trial will not be possible because you waive your rights under the terms of service in which you agreed at the time of setting up your online account. Do not agree to their terms of service when you create an account at their online services before you can request your free credit report. Forced arbitration clauses seldom help the consumer.

[7] Arbitration bias against the consumer in relation to credit bureaus refers to the fact that many consumer agreements include clauses that require disputes to be settled through arbitration rather than through the legal system. In many cases, these arbitration agreements are biased in favor of the credit bureaus and against the consumer, making it more difficult for individuals to challenge errors on their credit reports or hold the credit bureaus accountable for their actions. This can lead to a lack of transparency and accountability in the credit reporting industry.

You can only opt out of this particular clause by writing a letter within 30-60 days of creating your account to each credit reporting agency (see below the 3 credit bureau terms of service/arbitration clause below). It is advisable to do so by USPS certified mail in case you need to prove that you did opt out.

Transunion Arbitration Agreement

https://www.transunionplus.com/help/terms-and-privacy/site-use.htm#:~:text=Arbitration%20Agreement&text=If%20you%20bring%20a%20small,the%20applicable%20small%20claims%20court.

AGREEMENT TO RESOLVE DISPUTES BY BINDING INDIVIDUAL ARBITRATION

THIS SECTION IS AN AGREEMENT TO ARBITRATE DISPUTES ("**ARBITRATION AGREEMENT**") THAT MAY ARISE AS A RESULT OF YOUR TRANSUNION INTERACTIVE MEMBERSHIPS, PRODUCTS OR SERVICES OR THE AGREEMENT. READ THIS SECTION CAREFULLY. YOU UNDERSTAND AND AGREE THAT BOTH PARTIES WOULD HAVE HAD A RIGHT TO LITIGATE DISPUTES THROUGH A COURT AND TO HAVE A JUDGE OR JURY DECIDE THEIR CASE, BUT BOTH PARTIES BY ENTERING INTO THIS AGREEMENT CHOOSE TO HAVE ANY DISPUTE RESOLVED THROUGH BINDING INDIVIDUAL ARBITRATION. OTHER RIGHTS THAT YOU WOULD HAVE IF YOU WENT TO COURT MAY NOT BE AVAILABLE OR MAY BE MORE LIMITED IN ARBITRATION, INCLUDING YOUR RIGHT TO APPEAL.

RIGHT TO REJECT/OPT-OUT OF THE ARBITRATION AGREEMENT

YOU HAVE THE RIGHT TO REJECT THIS ARBITRATION AGREEMENT, BUT YOU MUST EXERCISE THIS RIGHT PROMPTLY. You must notify us in writing within sixty (60) days after the date you click-on to "Accept" the Agreement. You must send your request to: TransUnion Interactive, 100 Cross Street, Suite 202, San Luis Obispo, CA 93401. This request must include your current username and a clear statement of your intent, such as "I reject the arbitration clause in the TransUnion Interactive Service Agreement and Terms of Use."

Arbitration Agreement

In consideration for our willingness to provide you with access to products through the Site as set forth in the Agreement, you and we agree as follows:

If you bring small claims proceedings against TransUnion for money damages in an amount less than the statutory dollar limit for the small claims court in the applicable jurisdiction, then such claim will be resolved in the applicable small claims court.

If the amount you are claiming in damages in any court claim against TransUnion exceeds the dollar limit for small claims court in the applicable jurisdiction, then you agree that any dispute, claim or controversy ("**Claim**") between you and TransUnion Interactive or its parent, TransUnion, our agents, contractors, employees, officers or assignees, arising out of or relating in any way to this Agreement, your purchase and use of a TransUnion Interactive product or use of this Site, including, without limitation, tort and contract claims, claims based on any federal, state or local statute, law or regulation and the issue of arbitrability must be resolved exclusively by binding arbitration, except for the validity, scope or enforceability of this Arbitration Agreement. However, we will not demand arbitration pursuant to this Arbitration Agreement in connection with any individual Claim that you properly file and pursue in a small-claims court of your state or municipality, so long as the Claim is pending only in that court.

YOU UNDERSTAND AND AGREE THAT NO CLAIM, DISPUTE OR CONTROVERSY MAY BE CONSOLIDATED WITH A DISPUTE OF ANY OTHER PERSON IN ARBITRATION, OR RESOLVED ON A CLASS-WIDE BASIS BY A CLASS ACTION OR OTHER PROCEEDING AND YOU HEREBY WAIVE YOUR RIGHT TO COMMENCE OR PARTICIPATE IN ANY SUCH COLLECTIVE OR REPRESENTATIVE PROCEEDING. Unless a different procedure is required by applicable law, the arbitration will be conducted before a single arbitrator in accordance with the rules of the American Arbitration Association ("**AAA**"), including the AAA's Supplementary Procedures for Consumer-Related Disputes.

A demand for arbitration under this Arbitration Agreement may be made either before or after a lawsuit or other legal proceeding begins. However, any demand for arbitration that is made after a lawsuit or other legal proceeding has begun must be made within 90 days following the service of a complaint, third-party complaint, cross-claim or counterclaim or any answer thereto or any amendment to any of the above.

You understand and agree that before you take a dispute to arbitration under this Agreement, you must first contact our customer account representatives and give us an opportunity to resolve this dispute. Similarly, before TransUnion Interactive takes a dispute to arbitration, we must first attempt to resolve it by contacting you. If the dispute cannot be satisfactorily resolved within sixty days from the date you or TransUnion Interactive is notified of a dispute, either party may then contact the AAA in writing and request arbitration of the dispute. Information about the arbitration process and the AAA's arbitration rules and its fees are available from the AAA on the Internet at https://www.adr.org.

The cost of any arbitration proceeding shall be divided as follows:

- If you initiate arbitration, you will be responsible for paying one half of the filing fee, or $125.00, whichever is less, when the demand for arbitration is made.
- If we initiate arbitration, we will be responsible for paying all arbitration costs.
- Regardless of who initiates the arbitration, you will not be responsible for any arbitration fees that exceed one half of the filing fee, or $125.00, whichever is less, or the fees that you would have incurred if the Claim had been brought in court.

Experian Arbitration agreement:

https://www.experian.com/content/dam/marketing/na/assets/im/consumer-information/arbitration/ece-arbitration-agreement.pdf

Arbitration Agreement: (a) Experian and you agree to arbitrate all disputes and claims between us arising out of this Agreement directly related to the Service, Service Website, or its content, except any disputes or claims which under governing law are not subject to arbitration. This agreement to arbitrate is intended to be broadly interpreted and to make all disputes and claims between us directly relating to the provision of the Service, your use of the Service Website, or its content subject to arbitration to the fullest extent permitted by law. However, for the avoidance of doubt, any dispute you may have with us arising out of the Fair Credit Reporting Act ("FCRA") relating to the information contained in your consumer disclosure or report, including but not limited to claims for alleged inaccuracies, shall not be governed by this agreement to arbitrate. The agreement to arbitrate otherwise includes, but is not limited to: claims arising out of or relating to any aspect of the relationship between us arising out of the Service, Service Website, or its content, whether based in contract, tort, statute (including, without limitation, the Credit Repair Organizations Act) fraud, misrepresentation or any other legal theory; claims that arose before this or any prior Agreement (including, but not limited to, claims relating to advertising); claims that are currently the subject of purported class action litigation in which you are not a member of a certified class; and claims that may arise after the termination of this Agreement. For purposes of this arbitration provision, references to "Experian," "you," and "us" shall include our respective parent entities, subsidiaries, affiliates, agents, employees, predecessors in interest, successors and assigns, websites of the foregoing, as well as all authorized or unauthorized users or beneficiaries of services, products or information under this or prior Agreements between us relating to the Service, Service Website, or its content. Notwithstanding the foregoing, either party may bring an individual action in small claims court. You agree that, by entering into this Agreement, you and Experian are each waiving the right to a trial by jury or to participate in a class action. This Agreement evidences a transaction in interstate commerce, and thus the Federal Arbitration Act governs the interpretation and enforcement of this arbitration provision. This arbitration provision shall survive termination of this Agreement....

Equifax Arbitration Agreement:

https://www.equifax.com/terms/

AGREEMENT TO RESOLVE ALL DISPUTES BY BINDING INDIVIDUAL ARBITRATION. PLEASE READ THIS ENTIRE SECTION CAREFULLY BECAUSE IT AFFECTS YOUR LEGAL RIGHTS BY REQUIRING ARBITRATION OF DISPUTES (EXCEPT AS SET FORTH BELOW) AND A WAIVER OF THE ABILITY TO BRING OR PARTICIPATE IN A CLASS ACTION, CLASS ARBITRATION, OR OTHER REPRESENTATIVE ACTION. ARBITRATION PROVIDES A QUICK AND COST EFFECTIVE MECHANISM FOR RESOLVING DISPUTES, BUT YOU SHOULD BE AWARE THAT IT ALSO LIMITS YOUR RIGHTS TO DISCOVERY AND APPEAL.

Binding Arbitration. Any Claim (as defined below) raised by either You or Equifax against the other shall be subject to mandatory, binding arbitration. As used in this arbitration provision, the term "Claim" or "Claims" means any claim, dispute, or controversy between You and Us relating in any way to Your relationship with Equifax, including but not limited to any Claim arising from or relating to this Agreement, the Products or this Site, or any information You receive from Us, whether based on contract, statute, common law, regulation, ordinance, tort, or any other legal or equitable theory, regardless of what remedy is sought. This arbitration obligation extends to claims You may assert against Equifax's parents, subsidiaries, affiliates, successors, assigns, employees, and agents. The term "Claim" shall have the broadest possible construction, except that it does not include any claim, dispute or controversy in which You contend that EIS violated the FCRA. Any claim, dispute, or controversy in which You contend that EIS violated the FCRA is not subject to this provision and shall not be resolved by arbitration. The term "Claim" or "Claims" also does not apply to any claim, dispute, or controversy related to the TrustedID Premier product, www.equifaxsecurity2017.com, www.trustedidpremier.com, www.trustedid.com the Equifax cybersecurity incident announced on September 7, 2017, or to customers who were migrated from TrustedID Premier to an Equifax product.

No Class or Representative Arbitrations. The arbitration will be conducted as an individual arbitration. Neither You nor We consent or agree to any arbitration on a class or representative basis, and the arbitrator shall have no authority to proceed with arbitration on a class or representative basis. No arbitration will be consolidated with any other arbitration proceeding without the consent of all parties. This arbitration provision applies to and includes any Claims made and remedies sought as part of any class action, private attorney general action, or other representative action. By consenting to submit Your Claims to arbitration, You will be forfeiting Your right to bring or participate in any class action (whether as a named plaintiff or a class member) or to share in any class action awards, including class claims where a class has not yet been certified, even if the facts and circumstances upon which the Claims are based already occurred or existed.

Right to Opt-Out of this Arbitration Provision. IF YOU DO NOT WISH TO BE BOUND BY THE ARBITRATION PROVISION, YOU HAVE THE RIGHT TO EXCLUDE YOURSELF. Opting out of the arbitration provision will have no adverse effect on your relationship with Equifax or the delivery of Products to You by Equifax. In order to exclude Yourself from the arbitration provision, You must notify Equifax in writing within 30 days of the date that You first accept this Agreement on the Site (for Products purchased from Equifax on the Site). If You purchased Your Product other than on the Site, and thus this Agreement was mailed, emailed or otherwise delivered to You, then You must notify Equifax in writing within 30 days of the date that You receive this Agreement. To be effective, timely written notice of opt out must be delivered to Equifax Consumer Services LLC, Attn.: Arbitration Opt-Out, P.O. Box 105496, Atlanta, GA 30348, and must include Your name, address, and Equifax User ID, as well as a clear statement that You do not wish to resolve disputes with Equifax through arbitration. If You have previously notified Equifax that You wish to opt-out of arbitration, You are not required to do so again. Any opt-out request postmarked after the opt-out deadline or that fails to satisfy the other requirements above will not be valid, and You must pursue your Claim in arbitration or small claims court.

Initiation of Arbitration. Arbitration shall be administered by the American Arbitration Association ("AAA") under its Consumer Arbitration Rules in effect at the time the arbitration is filed unless any portion of those rules is inconsistent with any specific terms of this arbitration provision or this Agreement, in which case the terms of this arbitration provision and this Agreement will govern. The AAA's rules may be obtained at www.adr.org, or by calling the AAA at 1-88-778-7879. To commence an arbitration, you must file a copy of your written arbitration demand with the AAA (either online at www.adr.org or by mail addressed to AAA, Case Filing Services, 1101 Laurel Oak Road, Suite 100, Voorhees, NJ 08043). The arbitration shall be before a single arbitrator. The arbitrator will have the power to award a party any relief or remedy that the party could have received in court in accordance with the law or laws that apply to the dispute, subject to any limitations of liability or damages that exist under this Agreement. This agreement to arbitrate involves interstate commerce and is made pursuant to the Federal Arbitration Act, 9 U.S.C. sections 1-16 (the "FAA"). Any claim or dispute as to the enforceability of this arbitration provision's restrictions on your right to participate in or pursue a class action or class wide arbitration shall be decided by a court and not an arbitrator.

Payment of Arbitration Fees and Costs. In the event You file a Claim in arbitration in accordance with these provisions, We will advance all arbitration filing fees if You ask that We do so, in writing, prior to the commencement of the arbitration. The payment of any such fees will be made directly by Us to the AAA. Such requests should be mailed to Equifax Consumer Services LLC, Attn: Request for Payment of Arbitration Filing Fees, P.O. Box 105496, Atlanta, GA 30348. We will also pay all arbitrator fees. If Equifax prevails in the arbitration, then the arbitrator shall have the authority to require that You reimburse Equifax for the filing fees advanced, but only to the extent such fees would be recoverable by Us in a judicial action. You are responsible for all other fees and costs You incur in the arbitration, including attorney's fees and expert witness fees, except that the arbitrator shall have the authority to award attorney's fees and costs to the prevailing party; (i) based on applicable law; (ii) under the rules of the arbitration administrator; or (iii) if the arbitrator rules in Your favor and the arbitrator expressly determines that there is a good reason for requiring Us to pay those fees and costs.

OPT OUT OF FORCED ARBITRATION

Like I said before, you have a right to opt-out of the arbitration clause; however, it has to be recorded with the credit bureaus promptly. You must notify each credit bureau separately in writing within a specific time period after you click to "Accept" the agreement. My recommendation is to opt-out so you can go to a jury trial if you have to. Also, the profound reason to opt-out is that it will make your threat to sue real to the credit bureau because they will see that your account has rejected their arbitration clause.

If you threaten to sue but are still enrolled in their forced arbitration clause, you will not have the option of suing with a jury trial. Opting out of the forced arbitration agreement is your best bet in your credit repair journey. Here are the steps you need to take:

- Send a copy of the letter I provided to you *see below.
- Enclosed the identification form: Driver license, utility bill.
- Send the letter USPS certified mail.
- Only send to the address listed in their TOS for the opt-out. Do not use their corporate office or any other address you have found for the credit bureaus.
- Keep copies for your records and keep the mailing receipt.

Sample letter:

Your name

Address

City, State, Zip

S.S.#: 000-00-000 / D.O.B.: 01/01/1991

Experian/TransUnion/Equifax User ID:

Today's Date:

TransUnion

P.O. Box Address

City, State, Zip Code

To Whom It May Concern,

I have recently applied for an online account from Experian, TransUnion or Equifax. Please use this letter as confirmation that I wish not to be bound by the Arbitration clause under the terms of service. I do not wish to resolve disputes with you through arbitration.

In summary, I reject the arbitration clause under your terms of service.

Thank you for noting my account accordingly.

Sincerely,

Jane Doe

When you're ready to send your letter, make sure you do so using USPS certified mail with the US Postal service. Be sure to include the following copies along with your letter:

- S.S. card
- Utility bill
- Drivers license or Non-Driver license.

Equifax Consumer Services, LLC (30 days after you open online account)

Attn: Arbitration Opt-Out

P.O. Box 105496

Atlanta, GA 30348

TransUnion Interactive (60 days after you open online account)

P.O. Box 40

Woodlyn, PA 19094-0805

Experian Consumer Services (30 days after you open online account)

Attn: Arbitration Opt-Out

475 Anton Boulevard

Costa Mesa, CA 92626

To avoid being bound by an arbitration clause, it is recommended that you obtain a copy of your credit report from annualcreditreport.com instead of directly from the credit bureaus. This is because obtaining your credit report directly from the bureaus may require you to give up some of your official rights. However, it's worth noting that getting your credit report from annualcreditreport.com may take longer to resolve disputes, as it may take up to 45 days compared to the 30-day timeframe when getting your report directly from the credit bureaus. It's crucial to consider the pros and cons of each option when deciding from where to obtain your free credit report.

☞ **Credit tips:** As a responsible individual, it is imperative that you take the initiative to review your credit report and make sure that it is accurate. It is not uncommon for errors to occur on credit reports, and these errors could potentially harm your credit score and your chances of obtaining a loan or even a job. In fact, studies have shown that up to 80% of consumers may have errors on their credit reports without even realizing it. To prevent this from happening to you, it is important to regularly check your credit report and address any errors as soon as possible. By doing so, you can ensure that your credit score accurately reflects your credit solvency and increase your chances of obtaining favorable terms on loans, credit cards, and other financial products.

It is highly recommended that individuals make it a habit to review their credit reports regularly to ensure they recognize all charges and to identify any errors that could potentially harm their credit score. Just like reviewing monthly credit card statements, checking credit reports can help identify any adverse or damaging information that may be impacting credit scores. When reviewing your credit reports, it's a good idea to check for these common items:

CHECK FOR NEGATIVE MARKS

It's fundamental to regularly check your credit report for negative marks that do not belong to you. A credit report serves as a history of your behavior as a borrower, based on your accounts or trade lines. Trade lines are your credit accounts that report the type of account, date opened, credit limit or loan amount, account balance, and payment history. Basically, trade lines tell a story about your credit history to potential lenders, including the good, the bad, and everything in between.

Negative marks that don't belong to you or even those that can act as red flags to lenders when evaluating you for credit extension or increase. These marks can lower your credit score, and if too many are present, lenders may offer you more expensive products or outright reject your application. However, if you're aware of negative marks that don't belong to you, you can take steps to fix them and improve your credit.

When reviewing your credit report, look for any negative marks that don't belong to you, such as late payments or collection accounts that you didn't open. If you find any, you can dispute them with the credit bureaus by filing a dispute letter. You'll need to provide evidence that the negative mark is not yours, such as documentation showing the account wasn't opened by you or proof of payments made on time.

Disputing negative marks that don't belong to you is an important step in maintaining good credit. By being aware of these marks and taking action to fix them, you can ensure that your credit report accurately reflects your financial dependability to potential lenders. Below are what you should be looking for and the recommended solution:

- **Wrong personal information** – The first section of the report contains personal information. And so often, that's where the first errors are. One reason you want to make sure your credit profile contains accurate personal information is to prevent being a victim of identity theft or credit fraud. While your personal information doesn't impact your credit scores, it is still an important part of your credit profile as it is used to verify/substantiate a dispute. However, it is overall best to have updated personal information on your credit file. The information contained in your credit reports are based on the information obtained from the data creditors send to the bureaus.

☞ **Credit Tip:** In order to fix your credit the right way, you would want your credit profile to only contain 1 name, 1 address, 1 employer and make sure no misspelling on your name, no old/wrong addresses nor old employers etc... It is very important to have the credit bureaus update your personal information the right way.

- **Missing accounts** – This is huge. If an account isn't showing on your credit report or on-time payments are not being reported, this may be negatively impacting your credit score. There may be a mistake with your account and you want to correct information with the credit bureaus as soon as possible. You can expect a new credit card to show up on your credit report within a couple of months. The exact timing will depend on when the credit card company reports the information to the credit bureaus. If you happen to get a new credit account just after the company has reported to the credit bureaus, you may have to wait until the end of the next billing cycle for the information to appear on your credit report.

Tip: If you noticed a missing account, contact the creditor immediately and ask them for when they will report to the credit bureaus. This can easily be solved with the cooperation of the creditor. Since the creditor is the one that reports to the credit bureau, your only option is to contact them directly.

- **Accounts that do not belong to you** – Finding an unrecognized tradeline or account on your credit report can be troubling. This can have many implications with the main one being the possibility of identity theft or fraud. That's why it's wise to check your credit report often. The first step you need to take is to call the creditor immediately and ask to speak with a fraud specialist. Make sure to take detailed notes when you call, including the name of the rep, ID number and direct phone number of the representative that you talk to. Also be sure to inquire about the possibility of putting a freeze on the account in question if this is in fact an authorized account. This is important as it prevents new charges to the account while the account is being investigated for fraud.

☞ **Credit Tip:** If you're sure the new account does not belong to you, the next step would be removing it from your credit report. You would need to file a dispute letter with all the 3 credit bureaus. In addition, you would definitely want to put a credit freeze on your account for this not to be repeated. To dispute a new account that doesn't belong to you, I recommend you write to the credit bureaus as soon as possible to investigate this matter. The 3 credit bureaus disputing departments are listed below:

Credit Bureau	Dispute by Phone	Dispute Online	Dispute by Mail
TransUnion	1-800-916-8800	Start Below	TransUnion, LLC / P.O. Box 2000 / Chester, PA 19022
Equifax	1-866-349-5191	Start Below	Equifax Information Services, LLC / P.O. Box 740256 / Atlanta, GA 30374-0256
Experian	1-866-200-6020	Start Below	Experian / P.O. Box 4500 / Allen, TX 75013

*Transunion:	https://service.transunion.com/dss/login.page?dest=dispute
* Equifax:	https://www.equifax.com/personal/credit-report-services/credit-dispute/
* Experian:	https://www.experian.com/disputes/main.html

- **Incorrect dates** – If you identify an incorrect date on your credit report, notify the credit bureaus immediately. Explain in writing what you think is wrong in respect to the dates and remember to keep records of everything in your dispute process.

- **False Inquiries** – If you spot an unauthorized credit inquiry, this can be a clue to a bigger problem as it may be potentially identity theft or fraud. It is worth nothing that inquiries based on fraud can be fairly easy to remove if you provide proper proof. So stay vigilant and dispute the unauthorized inquiry.

☞ **Credit Tip:** If you suspect unauthorized credit inquiries on your credit report, here are five things you can do:

1. Contact the company that made the inquiry to remove the inquiry.

2. Report and document the fraud. You can go to the Federal Trade Commission's identityTheft.gov site where you can report an identity theft complaint to send to banks, creditors and the major credit bureaus. It is also recommended to file a police report which is required if you want to place an extended fraud alert on your credit profile.

3. Report and document the fraud to the credit bureaus. You can then decide to place a credit freeze to prevent further abuse of your credit report. You will need to contact all 3 credit bureaus to place the credit freeze.

4. Place a fraud alert immediately. You can place a free, 90 day fraud alert online with any of the credit bureaus. The alert serves to notify potential creditors to verify your identification prior to extending credit in your name.

5. Dispute the unauthorized inquiry with the credit bureaus. Once you report the unauthorized inquiry to the credit bureaus, they are required by law to investigate. I recommend you do not dispute the inquiry online but mailing your dispute.

- **Incorrect bankruptcies or foreclosures** – The impact of a bankruptcy or foreclosure on your credit report can be severe. The truth is both bankruptcy or foreclosure will cause your credit score to suffer. As you may know, bankruptcy is the worst of the bunch. It is highly recommended to check your credit file for incorrect bankruptcies or foreclosures as this will help you in your quest for good credit.
- **Duplicate accounts** – In some cases, errors by credit reporting agencies or creditors can result in duplication of accounts. If these duplicate entries are delinquent or reported as late accounts, this will cause your credit score to go down drastically. The duplication will cause double the negative impact on your credit score or creditworthiness. It is recommended to contact the creditor or the credit report agencies to fix the error.
- **Incorrect account status, delinquencies or derogatory marks.** For example, an account is closed when in fact it's supposed to be open or late 90 days when it should only be late 60 or 30 days etc... You can contact the business providing the incorrect information. It must then inform the bureaus of the dispute and if it finds the information to be wrong or incomplete, it must be deleted.

Overall, if you see items on your credit report that are either not accurate or don't belong to you, you have a right in line with the fair credit act to dispute it. The credit report agency has a duty by law to order an investigation. You can dispute the item either online or in writing. I recommend you do so in writing, not online. You can write a letter to the credit bureau using USPS certified mail.

When you dispute an item, credit reporting agencies are required by law to verify that information with the creditor within 30 days. They are allotted an additional 15 days if they get data from credit issuing agencies. In total the credit reporting agency has 45 days to start and complete the investigation and to inform you of the outcome.

The Fair Credit Act states that any item that cannot be verified must be deleted immediately. It is your responsibility to take charge of fixing your credit once and for all. You are the only person who truly cares about your credit, so you need to take matters into your own hands. Congratulations on buying this book, but now it's time to move on to the next phase and proactively work on fixing your credit. Besides checking for negative marks, there are other items to look for in your report that greatly impact your score.

CHECK FOR DEROGATORY MARKS

A derogatory mark is a negative item, such as a late payment, accounts collection account, charge-off and so on.... These derogatory marks are typically on accounts that are 30 days or more past due or items that are considered a credit risk like bankruptcy. If a negative mark or derogatory mark is showing on your credit reports, it can hurt your credit scores and affect your chances of qualifying for credit cards, loans and mortgages. These negative items have what's known as *statute of limitations as outlined in the Fair Credit Reporting Act. So rest assured that the negative marks do have an expiration date so to speak. These derogatory marks can stay on your credit reports up to seven to 10 years depending on the type of mark but generally their impact on your credit diminishes over time. Below I will discuss the different types of negative marks that impact your credit score.

* Understanding the statute of limitations for debts in your state is a crucial factor that can affect your credit report in ways you may not have anticipated. The statute of limitations can differ from state to state, making it necessary for you to do a bit of research. However, once you have that information, you'll be able to make wise decisions about your debts.

For instance, let's say the statute of limitations in your state is seven years and you're in the sixth year. It's advantageous to know that any payments made before the expiration of the statute of limitations will reset the clock. This means that if you make a payment during the sixth year, the clock resets, and you have another six years to deal with the debt.

It's crucial to exercise caution when paying off old debts, especially if the statute of limitations is about to expire. Waiting until the statute of limitations has run out before sending a letter to the credit reporting agencies may be a better option for you. This will ensure that you don't restart the clock on the statute of limitations, which could lead to a longer period of time to deal with the debt.

Overall, understanding the statute of limitations is an important factor when dealing with debts, and taking the time to research it will help you make informed choices.

CHECK FOR LATE PAYMENTS

Late payments are usually not reported until 30 days after the due date and will remain on your credit report for the duration of the statute of limitations, which is 7 years.

<u>What to do:</u>

1. **Make a payment as soon as possible** – Payment history is the most important part of your credit score which accounts up to 35% of your total score. A late payment is the fastest way to hurt your score. The longer the payment is late, the more it hurts your score. So please make a payment as soon as possible. If money is scarce at this time, the minimum is to make the minimum payment.
2. **Ask for a "Goodwill Adjustment"**- Go ahead, call your credit card company and ask them as a courtesy to remove late payments or other fees. You will be surprised how you can get a Goodwill adjustment by simply calling your credit card company and asking them to help you out.

(Sample goodwill letter)

To Whom It May Concern,

Thank you for taking the time to read this letter. I'm writing because I noticed that my most recent credit report contains a late payment reported on () for my account.

I want you to know that I understand my financial obligations and if it weren't for (circumstance that caused you to miss payment(s)), I'd have an excellent repayment record with your company. I made a mistake in falling behind, but since then, (described the positive change in circumstance). Since then, I've had a spotless record of on-time payments.

I'm planning to apply for a (mortgage....), and it's come to my attention that the missed payment(s) on my record could hurt my ability to qualify. I truly believe that it doesn't reflect my creditworthiness and commitment to repaying my debts. It would help me tremendously if you could give me a second chance and make a goodwill adjustment to remove the late payment(s) as referenced above.

Thank you for your consideration, and I hope and pray that you will approve my request.

Sincerely,

Your name

1- **Sign Auto Payments** - You can negotiate removal of late payments by signing up for Auto Payments. By the way, all your accounts should be set up for Auto Payments. That way, you will never be late on a credit card payment ever again. You can set up Auto Payment by taking the minimum payment each month. You can always make extra payments in case your financial situation becomes fruitful. This doesn't work all the time but it doesn't hurt to try. So go ahead, call your credit card company and give it a try.

2- **Remember that the creditors are humans** - Always keep in touch with your lender and express your unfortunate financial situation to see if it is possible to reduce the debt or come to an agreement. The creditors want to get their money back and some will try to work with you to come up with some type of resolution.

CHECK FOR COLLECTION ACCOUNTS

This is basically unpaid debt that is sold to collection agencies for pennies on the dollar. These accounts hurt your score a lot. You don't want to have any collection accounts. Credit reporting agencies collect public record information from state and county courts and information on overdue debt from different collection agencies. Collections typically happen after 5 to 6 months of late payments and should only stay on your report for 7 years. But that can vary if the collection company reinstate the account after an event or if you decided to pay the credit before the statute of limitations. Hence, restart the clock so to speak. In general, the statute of limitations for collection accounts is 7 years.

What to do:

1- **Be proactive and dispute all collection/charge-off accounts:** You want to make sure there are not any errors in reporting. You want to check for things such as a wrong account number, outdated status, a wrong date of delinquency or a date past 7 years. Remember, collection accounts are only supposed to be reported for 7 years. So make sure you check that there aren't any accounts past the 7 years threshold.

2- **You can ask for a goodwill deletion:** Go ahead and call the original creditor or send a letter to them explaining your financial trouble and ask them if they can delete the collection again as a goodwill. A well written letter may do the trick. Again, it doesn't hurt to ask.

3- **Write a pay to delete Letter:** You can explain in your letter that you will pay the debt if they agree to remove the debt from your credit report. You can either pay in full or try to negotiate a lesser amount of the debt. Some collection agencies will accommodate you. Make sure you get things in writing and only pay if you have a letter in hand explaining exactly what will be done. This letter can be a contract between you and the original creditor.

4- **You can ask for a lower payoff:** Most debts are bought for pennies on the dollar. So it's worth a try to ask the collection agencies to take a lesser amount than the original debt. Explain your financial difficulties and that you don't have the money to pay the full amount and ask them if you can negotiate a lesser amount. This is a win-win situation as the collection agencies want to get some type of compensation for the debts to stay in business and you want the collection agencies to remove the collection account from your credit report in order for you to have a better credit score. It's a win-win situation for all parties involved. You can request a lowering of the debt by let's say 40% to 50% or even 60%. It can be done and all you have to do is negotiate the best percentage for yourself. And remember to always get things in writing before you pay anything. Please keep in mind if you are close to 7 years, it doesn't pay to negotiate the account. The best thing to do is to wait out the 7 years when the debt will automatically be deleted from your credit report.

CHECK FOR ACCOUNT CHARGE-OFFS

After a period of time after you fail to resolve or pay the debt or can not pay the lender, the account will simply go into charge off by the creditor. In other words, the creditor will take the account off their books and will usually sell the account to a collection company for pennies on the dollar. Again, the account charge off should stay on your credit for 7 years.

What to do:

1- If the lender hasn't sold the account, you can offer to pay in full for the charge-off to be removed from your report or you can negotiate a pay-for-delete agreement for a lesser amount.

2- If it was sold, you will have to deal with the credit collectors which you may do the same as outlined in item 1.

3- If the charge-off is inaccurate, write a letter to the bureaus of the error. Follow the same steps outlined in Collection Account.

CHECK FOR HARD INQUIRIES

A hard inquiry appears on your credit after you have made an attempt to obtain credit. It doesn't matter if you were approved or denied for the loan. The hard inquiry will appear as a way to tell the CRA that you tried to add more loans/credit to your profile. Hard inquiries stay on your credit report for a maximum of 2 years.

CHECK FOR HIGH UTILIZATION RATE

When it comes to your credit score, high utilization is considered using more than 30% of your total credit limit. For example: if your credit limit is $1,000 then your balance should be $300 or less. Anything above $300 would be considered high utilization which hurts your score. Of course, the higher the credit utilization, the worse it is for the consumer. So keeping your credit utilization under 30% is the goal and key to a higher credit score.

What to do:

1. **Find out when your issuer reports.** Every credit card reports every 30 days but the billing date and reporting date might be different. When you have the correct date, you will know when and how often to pay your credit card to show the best utilization rate for each reporting period.

2. **Ask for an increased credit limit.** You should be asking for an increased credit limit every 6 months. There are times when the credit card company will automatically increase your credit line. It doesn't happen often but it does happen. But it never hurts to call them or go online and request a credit limit increase. If your credit limit increases, it automatically reduces your credit utilization rate. Make sure there's no hard inquiry on your credit profile or else this will hurt your score. Imagine if you were denied but yet there's an additional hard inquiry on your credit profile. This would not be beneficial for your goal to have good credit. So tread lightly. The best thing is to make sure you have a high chance of getting approved if a hard inquiry will be part of the process.

3. **Ask to be an authorized user on someone else's credit card.** This will lower your overall utilization rate as the new card will be utilized as additional credit. Hence, lowering your

overall credit utilization rate. The ideal candidate is someone consistently making on-time payments and someone with a lengthy account history of at least 2 years or more.

4. **Open a new credit card.** When you open a new credit card, you automatically increase your credit line. Hence, the new card helps to automatically decrease your overall credit utilization rate. The downside in applying for a new card is that it will always trigger a hard inquiry on your credit report. I don't recommend this step unless you have a lengthy credit history and you are confident that you will be qualified for the new card. Again, tread lightly.

5. **Do not close unused cards.** Closing a card that you are not using will cause your credit utilization rate to go up. Think about it; if you have a $1,000 credit card that you're not using, then if you close it then that's $1,000 less in your available credit. Hence, your credit utilization equation will be adversely affected.

CHECK FOR REPOSSESSION

When you can't pay for an item such as a car, the lender or the bank has the right to repossess the vehicle which in turn hurts your credit score tremendously. In layman's turn, when the lender repossesses your car, it means that the lender is taking back the car because you were not able to meet your financial obligation. There are various fees associated with a repossession, not to mention the adverse impact on your credit score. Like other items, repossession will stay on your credit report for 7 years and the negative impact can be devastating.

<u>What to do:</u>

1. The Fair Credit Reporting Act requires that all negative marks like repossession be true. Hence only real past-due accounts can be listed on your report.
2. If the repossession was an error, you have a right to dispute it right away.
3. You can contact the lender to see if you can negotiate debt or pay to delete the agreement.

CHECK FOR STUDENT LOAN DELINQUENCY OR DEFAULT

Student loan delinquency occurs when a borrower fails to make a loan payment by its due date. After a certain period of delinquency, the loan will be considered in default. Defaulting on a student loan can have serious consequences, such as damage to credit score, wage garnishment, and even judicial action. It is important to stay on top of student loan payments and communicate with the lender if there are any difficulties in making payments. Student loan delinquencies stay on your credit report for 7 years. You can follow up with the lender to make a payment plan to bring the account current.

What to do:

1. Make sure to understand the terms of your student loan and repayment plan.
2. Set up automatic payments or reminders to ensure you don't miss a payment.

3. Communicate with your loan servicer if you are experiencing financial difficulties or need to change your repayment plan.
4. Consider enrolling in an income-driven repayment plan, which adjusts your payments based on your income and family size.
5. Explore options for deferment or forbearance if you are experiencing a temporary financial hardship.
6. If this is an error, follow the steps previously outlined to dispute this item.

CHECK FOR BANKRUPTCY

Bankruptcy is a legal process that provides individuals and businesses with relief from their debts by either restructuring their payment plans or discharging their debts altogether. It is usually considered a last resort when other debt repayment options are not feasible. Bankruptcy can impact a person's credit score and make it more difficult to obtain credit in the future, but it can also provide a fresh start for those struggling with overwhelming debt.

Different types of bankruptcy will stay on your credit report for different lengths of time. Chapter 13 and chapter 7 have different statute of limitations.

Chapter 13 – Stays on your credit report for 7 years.

Chapter 7 – Stays on your credit report for 10 years.

* See our bonus book about bankruptcy.

CHECK FOR FORECLOSURES OR SHORT SALE

Foreclosure is a legal process that allows a lender to seize and sell a property when the borrower defaults on their mortgage payments. It is a serious and often traumatic event for homeowners that can have long-lasting financial consequences. On the other hand, a short sale is a type of real estate transaction in which the lender agrees to accept less than the full amount owed on the mortgage, allowing the homeowner to sell the property and avoid foreclosure.

Foreclosures stay on your credit report for 7 years. To dispute any errors in reporting, follow the steps outlined earlier.

CHECK FOR PUBLIC UTILITIES AND MEDICAL BILLS

Credit reports are critical documents that provide an overview of your credit history, and they are used by lenders and creditors to evaluate your creditworthiness. However, it is important to understand that credit reports do not include all types of debt, such as public utilities and medical bills. These types of bills typically do not appear on your credit report, but there are exceptions to this rule.

For example, if you fail to pay your utility bills on time and they go into default, the utility company may report the delinquent account to credit bureaus, which will then show up on your credit report. Similarly, if you fail to pay your medical bills, the provider may sell the debt to a collection agency, which will then report it to the credit bureaus. These types of bills can be detrimental to your credit score, as they can lower your overall score and make it more difficult to obtain credit in the future.

Debt collectors and collection agencies use credit reports as a tool to motivate consumers to pay off their debts or negotiate a settlement. They understand that most people value their credit scores and want to maintain good credit, so they use the threat of damaging credit reports to get consumers to pay up. If you have any delinquent utility or medical bills, it is important to address them promptly and work with the service provider or collection agency to resolve the issue before it shows up on your credit report.

In summary, while public utilities and medical bills typically do not appear on credit reports, there are situations where they can. Therefore, it is to your advantage to stay on top of these bills and address any delinquencies promptly to avoid damaging your credit score. If you do happen to see a public utilities or medical bill on your credit report that you believe is in error, it's valuable to follow the steps outlined for disputing errors in credit reporting to ensure accuracy and fairness in your credit history.

WATCHDOG = CREDIT MONITORING

I strongly recommend you get a credit monitoring service to act like a watchdog over your credit file and notify you of any changes to your credit report so you can act quickly to avert further damages. Credit monitoring is extremely important against identity theft. In today's world, having control of your credit can help you save time and money. You can think of credit monitoring as having a personal assistant to your credit profile but also as a guardian. It watches your credit reports and will alert you of any changes or suspicious activities to any of your accounts. The credit monitoring will alert you of fraudsters opening accounts in your name which will typically show up within 30 days on your credit report especially when they fail to make payments on these accounts. While it is true that credit monitoring will only catch the thievery after a fraudulent account has been opened under your name; however, it is important to catch the fraudster as soon as possible to mitigate the damages.

Another benefit of having credit monitoring is also to help you monitor the progress of your credit repair journey. Keeping tabs on your credit report can show you your progress on your credit repair so that you know where your credit stands. This is a win-win situation of using credit monitoring services and I can stress the importance of having credit monitoring services. This is an absolute must for fixing your credit or building your credit or just to have the peace of mind that your credit has not been compromised. There are many credit monitoring services offering different services and different price points. I encourage you to do a search on the internet for "best credit monitoring services" and then you can make your choice based on your comfortability level with both service and price point. Below are two credit monitoring companies that I recommend:

CreditKarma- You can access both your TransUnion and Equifax FICO score for free using CreditKarma.com. The best part of this service is that it is absolutely free. Credit Karma uses the VantageScore 3.0 model that uses scores ranging from 300 to 850. Credit Karma is an online credit service that gives you access to your credit score for free whenever you'd like without paying any fees. You'll need to sign up for the service only and you can instantly begin to monitor your credit profile.

IdentityIQ – You can access all your three credit bureaus credit reports on this site. You can get your credit scores from Experian,

TransUnion and Equifax when you sign up. This is a subscription based service. However, there's always a promotional trial running usually $1 for a 7 day trial. Then, as low as $9.99 per month depending on the plan you choose.

Experian – You can access your Experian score by subscription only. You can start with an introductory price of $4.95 for your first month of access, then you can pay about $19.95 each additional month. You have the option of canceling at any time if you're not satisfied. Experian uses the FICO score 8 model and the scores range from 250-900.

STEP 2:

Freeze your secondary credit reporting agencies: This is the secret sauce. To maximize the effectiveness of your credit repair efforts, it is highly recommended that you freeze your secondary credit reporting agencies prior to disputing any items on your credit report. By doing so, you can prevent any new negative information from being added to your credit report while you work to remove existing negative items.

To clarify, secondary credit reporting agencies are those that are not among the big three collection agencies (Equifax, Experian, and TransUnion) but still gather and report credit information. Examples of secondary credit reporting agencies include Innovis, PRBC, and SageStream.

Freezing your secondary credit reporting agencies involves contacting each agency and requesting a security freeze be placed on your credit report. This will prevent any new accounts or credit inquiries from being added to your report without your authorization.

Repairing your credit can be done in different ways, but there are effective and ineffective methods. To improve your credit score, it's worthwhile to choose the right approach. Some strategies may not yield the desired results or may even cause further damage to your credit. Therefore, it's key to understand the proper way of repairing your credit to achieve a positive outcome. A sure way to fail in your credit repair journey is to download a template dispute letter better known as a 609 letter and just blast it out to the credit bureaus. Sometimes, consumers pay upwards of $75 to even hundreds of dollars for some proprietary dispute letters that were crafted or created by attorneys or credit repair companies... What often happens is that you send out these fancy letters and then everything comes back as verified and that does little to move the needle on your credit score.

This process just doesn't work and people often get frustrated and give up in the process. As we learned from chapter 1, the dispute letters get scanned by a computer and assigned a 3 digits letter from the e-Oscar system. You should know by now from reading this book that nobody is actually going to read your dispute letter in the first place. Hence, it should be crystal clear that a template letter that you sent to dispute your items does not matter. Under any circumstance do not pay for these proprietary dispute letters. Stop wasting your hard earned money on buying expensive dispute letters. Instead, do what is outlined in this book and that will dramatically increase your odds of success.

The most effective way to be on the right track of fixing your credit is to place a security freeze on your credit file. Based on the Fair Credit Act, you have a right to place a security freeze on your credit report. A credit freeze has multiple applications including preventing fraudulent credit applications and or prevention of identity theft even though a criminal has your birthdate and social security number... But for the purpose of this book, a credit freeze is the secret sauce in fixing your credit. A credit freeze in place will make the credit bureaus unable to validate negative items on your credit report. That way, you are making it extremely difficult for E-OSCAR to have access to the data that they need to actually validate the disputed negative items on your credit report. By law, if they are unable to verify or validate a negative item in a specific time frame, then it must be deleted.

Before we begin, I would like to state with certainty that a credit freeze is harmless. What credit repair agencies or the establishments don't want you to know is that you can do a credit freeze yourself. The great credit repair myth will be dispelled once and for all. The guiding principle of a credit freeze or a security freeze is to protect you from identity theft or prevent further misuse of your personal information if it was stolen. The main purpose of a credit freeze is clear; a credit freeze is an anti-fraud measure in which a credit bureau or the secondary credit reporting agency (CRA) refrains from sharing your credit report with any third party without your consent. Now what most people don't know is that a credit freeze does more than what I just explained.

The credit repair services in the US is a big business. It is expected to gross 4.4Bn in revenue in the year 2022. Since we established that the scope of the credit repair services is big in nature, I would now share with you some tactics that the most successful credit repair company uses to delete items on a consumer's credit. The strategies presented forth are industry's secrets and the cost is minimal to you compared to subscriptions fees amounting to billions of dollars consumers pay to the credit repair companies year after year. I am here to empower the consumers to retake their powers back. I am here not necessary to bankrupt the credit repair companies but to even out the playing field.

My main objective for writing this book is to make credit repair not only available to those who can afford paying credit repair companies but also available to the average consumer void of a big bank account. Armed with the proper knowledge, anyone can fix their credit report by themselves. A sure way to begin the credit repair journey to ensure the best chance of success is to study the Fair Credit Act and to apply a credit freeze prior to disputing any items on your credit report. That's right. The most successful credit repair companies use that little trick using a credit freeze on their client's credit report and this is completely legitimate.

Credit freeze is a powerful tool that consumers can use to protect themselves from fraud and identity theft. According to the Fair Credit Reporting Act, every individual has the right to place a credit or security freeze on their credit report. By doing so, you can prevent unauthorized access to your credit report and mitigate the damage in case you become a victim of identity theft.

Credit repair companies also use credit freeze to delete negative items on your credit report. When you dispute an item on your credit report, the credit bureaus are required by law to verify the item in question. If they are unable to do so, then the item must be deleted. This is where credit freeze comes into play. By preventing the credit bureaus from accessing your credit file from third-party data collecting agencies, credit freeze can make it difficult for them to verify disputed items.

This strategy is similar to Johnny Cohran's famous closing statement in the O.J. Simpson trial, "If it doesn't fit, you must acquit." In other words, if the information cannot be verified, then it must be deleted. This can work wonders for your credit score, as negative items that are deleted from your credit report can significantly improve your credit strength.

However, it is important to note that credit freeze should be used responsibly and only for legitimate reasons. Misusing credit freeze can result in unintended consequences, such as delays in obtaining credit or loans. Therefore, it is vital to weigh the pros and cons and seek professional advice before putting a credit freeze in place.

HOW DOES A CREDIT FREEZE REALLY WORK

As a consumer, you have the right to implement a security freeze on your credit report conforming to the Fair Credit Reporting Act. The credit freeze serves various purposes such as controlling who has access to your credit report and preventing credit fraud or identity theft. However, it's critical to keep in mind that a credit freeze may create some delays, interference or even prohibit timely approval of new loans, credit, mortgage applications or accounts that involve the extension of credit. This is due to the additional steps that need to be taken to temporarily lift or permanently remove the security freeze. Nevertheless, these minor inconveniences are outweighed by the benefits that a credit freeze provides for consumers.

Let's say you have a dispute with an incorrect item on your credit report. You write a letter to the credit bureau about the issue. The credit bureau by law has to investigate this item. Don't worry, Sherlock Holmes will not be doing the investigation. Instead, the credit bureau will hire one of the many secondary credit reporting agencies to conduct the investigation. The main purpose of the CRA when conducting the investigation is to match the account to you or to validate the account to the consumer. So they don't need the original sign application, rate disclosure and so on... They just need to somehow link you to the account. If the account is able to be verified then that's the end of the story. The account will come back as "verify" with no changes to your credit report. What you want to do is block the secondary credit reporting agency from accessing your credit report. That way, the information or your dispute can not be verified in most cases. Hence, drastically increases your odds of getting this item deleted from your credit report. In the next chapter, I will outline the secondary credit report agencies which you also need to block from accessing your credit file.

Secondary credit reporting agencies, just like the big three credit reporting companies, possess valuable information that identity thieves seek. They hold important details such as your social security number, birthdate, and driver's license number, along with personal information that can be used to authenticate your accounts during a dispute.

THE CREDIT FREEZE PROCESS EXPLAINED

The credit freeze process is usually the same with the 3 major credit bureaus and all secondary reporting companies. You'll need to file a credit freeze request for it to be effective. During the process, you'll need to answer questions to verify your identity. In all cases, you'll need to provide your Social Security number, a copy of a photo ID and proof of residence, such as a recent utility bill. In the age of computers and online services, you may be able to create an account online that you can use to freeze and unfreeze your credit file.

If you intend to apply for credit while a credit freeze is active on your credit report, you will need to lift the freeze temporarily or permanently to enable the lender to access your credit report during its routine credit check. To prevent the secondary credit reporting agencies from accessing your credit file, here is a list of the companies you should block. Additionally, I have provided instructions on how to block the three major credit bureaus. See illustration below:

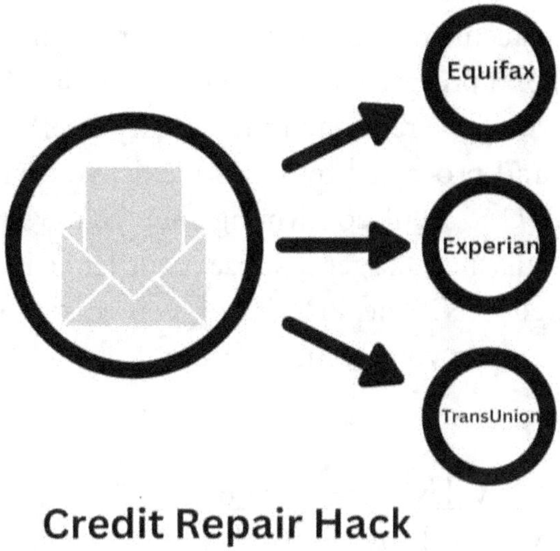

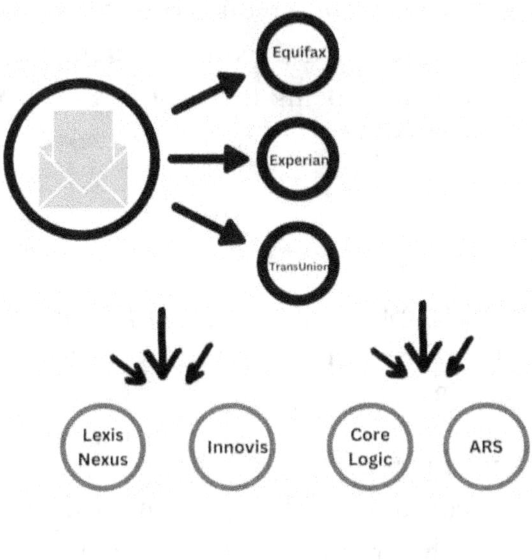

Lexis Nexis – This credit reporting company collects data on real estate transactions and ownership data, lien, judgment and bankruptcy records, professional license information and historical addresses. You can request your security freeze, or temporarily lift or permanently remove your security freeze, as well as order a replacement PIN for yourself or a minor child (under the age of 16) or a protected consumer using online Security Freeze Forms. Once you have requested the security freeze and once it has been verified and processed by Lexis Nexis, you will then receive a letter in the U.S. Mail confirming that your request has been completed. You will then get a subsequent letter in the mail with your designated PIN. The PIN is for you to temporarily lift or permanently remove your security freeze.

What to do:

Go to: https://www.lexisnexis.com/privacy/fo... or you can type a search query on your browser for "Lexis Nexis credit freeze". Or you can call them at 800-456-1244.

Sage Stream – As part of LexisNexis Risk Solutions, this company provides consumer reports and credit scores to different types of companies including credit card issuers, retailers and wireless telephone service providers. Being that SageStream is now part of LexisNexis, follow the steps above to also freeze your SageStream credit report.

What to do:

Go to: https://www.sagestreamllc.com/securit... or you can type a search query on your browser for "SageStream credit freeze". Or you can call them at 888-395-0277.

Innovis – This company is often referred to as the 4th largest credit bureau, supplying consumer data to credit card companies and other businesses. The report includes your credit history, consisting of accounts you have now or have had in the past. Also, the report includes personal identification information such as your name, address, date of birth and contact information on file. A credit freeze prevents your Innovis credit report from being accessed by most third parties in connection with a credit application for new credit. With a security freeze in place you will need to take special steps when you wish to apply for any type of credit. A security freeze will be placed on the credit report after your request has been received and your identity has been verified by Innovis.

What to do:

You can request a credit freeze on the company's website, by mail, by phone or in person, at its Pittsburgh headquarters. https://www.innovis.com/securityFreez... or you can type a search query on your browser for "Innovis credit freeze". Or you can call them at 866-712-4546.

Corelogic Teletrack– This is one of the consumer reporting companies in the United States. This company collects and reports personal data such as property ownership and home loan obligations record; property legal filings and tax payment status; rental applications and collection accounts; consumer bankruptcies, liens, judgments, and child support obligations. Again, you have a right in accordance with the Fair Credit Act to put a credit freeze on your credit profile. By placing a security freeze on your CoreLogic Teletrack consumer report, banks and other companies will not be able to access your credit report.

What to do:

To place a credit freeze with Corelogic, you can either call the firm or fill out a form, which is provided on its website, and fax it in, along with identifying information. https://www.innovis.com/securityFreez... or you can type a search query on your browser for "Innovis credit freeze". Or you can call them at 866-712-4546.

Advanced Resolution Services (ARS) – This company collects debt collection accounts information on consumers credit reports. Under the Fair Credit Reporting Act, you have a right to obtain a security freeze of your credit report from ARS. Adding a security freeze with ARS restricts access to your credit information and the information can not be published to the credit bureaus. When a security freeze is added, a Personal Identification Number (PIN) is provided to you. You will be required to provide this PIN to suspend or remove the credit freeze from your credit report in the future.

What to do:

Go to: https://www.ars-consumeroffice.com/se... or you can type a search query on your browser for "ARS credit freeze". Or you can call them at 800-392-8911.

ChexSystems- This company was founded in 1971. It reports to financial institutions when you apply for a new bank account. This company collects Social Security numbers, addresses and birthdays, as well as information about former residences, bank accounts and retail transactions. You can order your consumer report as well as request a credit freeze directly through the firm's website. Please note that some information can still be shared even with a credit freeze. If you owned an account that was closed with substantial overdrafts, ATM abuse or fraud, ChexSystems can release that information to banks or other financial institutions reviewing your application for a checking or savings account.

What to do:

You must be 18 years of age or older to communicate with ChexSystems. To place a security freeze on your file, you will receive a unique PIN by mail. The PIN will be required to perform specific actions with regards to applying a temporary lift or removing or changing personal identifying information like changing address, social security number and so on...). You can place a security freeze via website, phone or mail. https://www.chexsystems.com/security-freeze/place-freeze or you can type a search query on your browser for "ChexSystems credit freeze". Or you can call them at 800-887-7652. ChexSystems, Inc. Attn: Security Freeze Department P.O. Box 583399 Minneapolis, MN 55458.

Clarity Services – This company is owned by Experian and provides financial data to more than 62 million U.S. consumers. Clarity Services is a federally regulated credit bureau that analyzes data on mostly non-prime credit ratings. Clarity Services was founded in 2008 to provide credit risk analysis to financial institutions that services the subprime market. The company collects and provides information on payday loans, installment loans, auto loans (and leasing), check cashing services, rent-to-own transactions, telecommunication account openings, and financial services with an emphasis on the lower income and subprime market segments.

What to do:

You can place a security freeze via website, phone or mail: https://consumers.clarityservices.com/securityfreeze or you can type a search query on your browser for "Clarity Services credit freeze". Or you can call them at 866-390-3118. Mailing address: Clarity Services, Inc. Consumer Support Division P.O. Box 16 Allen, TX 75013.

- **Equifax:** Call 800-349-9960 or go online. Check out our step-by-step Equifax credit freeze guide.
- **Experian:** Call 888-397-3742 or go online. Here's a detailed walk-through on getting an Experian credit freeze.

- **TransUnion:** Call 888-909-8872 or go online. Read our TransUnion credit freeze guide.

CREDIT FREEZE EXEMPTION

Even with a credit freeze in place, certain third parties can still have access to your Credit Report pursuant to the Fair Credit Reporting Act. This include the following entities:

- Companies that have current accounts or relationships with you.
- Collection agencies acting on behalf of companies that have a current account or existing relationship with you.
- Credit monitoring companies.
- State or local agencies including law enforcement or child support agencies.
- Federal government agencies as permitted conforming to the Fair Credit Reporting Act.

STEP 3:

Prepare your letters for success: This is the actual disputing process- Let the war begin.

Having a credit freeze is of utmost importance when it comes to disputing any item on your credit report. Without it, you are ultimately wasting your time. In just a matter of seconds, e-Oscar can verify a disputed item and return all your items as "verified."

If you persist by writing subsequent letters, you run the risk of being labeled as a "Frivolous claim." This can severely limit your options, leaving you with no choice but to either pay the debt or wait until the statute of limitations has expired. Therefore, it cannot be emphasized enough how crucial it is to have a credit freeze in place prior to disputing any item on your report.

Your very first letter: To initiate the dispute process effectively, it is highly recommended to first rectify any errors in the personal information section of your credit report. The importance of this step cannot be overstated, as even minor discrepancies in your name, address, or other personal details can result in inaccurate reporting of credit accounts and negatively impact your credit score. Therefore, it is crucial to carefully review your personal information section and ensure that all details are correct and up-to-date. Once this step is completed, you can proceed with confidence to address any disputed items in your credit report.

In order to ensure the accuracy of your credit report, it's imperative to start by reviewing and correcting any errors in your personal information section. This involves removing any excess personal identifiers such as old addresses, names, and employers. It's recommended that you contact the credit bureaus either by phone or through a written letter to request the removal of these extra identifiers. Simplify your personal information to have only one name, one address, and one employer.

Removing excess personal identifiers is an important step to make your credit repair process easier. Keeping old names, addresses, or employers in your credit profile can lead to the verification of an old account, making it difficult to dispute and remove adverse accounts. The credit bureaus' goal is to link accounts to you, so removing all but one name, address, and employer can aid in the dispute process and increase your chances of removing negative accounts from your credit report.

What you need to do:

Send out a USPS certified letter to all 3 credit bureaus saying that this is my name, address, employer and telephone numbers. Please remove all other names and addresses and other items from my personal history as I might be susceptible to identity theft. That's all you have to do. It does not need to be fancy or contain a lot of legal terminologies and it certainly doesn't have to come from a lawyer. You need to type your name and do not wet sign your signature as this can be a source of verification.

Sample letter:

Your name

Address

City, State, Zip

S.S.#: 000-00-000 / D.O.B.: 01/01/1991

Today's Date:

TransUnion

P.O. Box Address

City, State, Zip Code

To Whom It May Concern,

This is my official request to update my personal information on my credit report.

My name is: Jane Doe

My address is listed above

My telephone number is 212 123-4567

My current employer is: ABC Corporation.

Please remove all other names and addresses and other items from my personal history as I might be susceptible to identity theft.

I thank you in advance for updating my account.

Sincerely,

*Jane Doe

---

* Do not wet sign your signature as this may be used to verify an account.

Be sure to always include the following documents to establish your identity and place of residence of all communications with the credit bureaus:

- Copy driver license or Non-Driver license
- Utility bill: gas or electric...
- S.S. card

Why USP Certified mail?

USPS Certified mail contains a timestamp when the letter went out and delivered. By law, credit bureaus only have a certain time period to investigate and to make a decision to update the item or comply with your request. If not, you can easily sue them for non-compliance and in a nutshell breaking the law by violating your rights under the Fair Credit Reporting Act. You can sue them in small claims court and you don't need a lawyer. You can do it yourself and you are pretty much guaranteed monetary compensation with the appropriate proof.

Remember, by law, the credit bureaus have 30 days (an additional 15 days if they get information from the actual credit issuing agencies) from start to finish to complete their investigative process and to either verify or remove the item(s) from your credit report. If they don't, on the 46th day, you can easily sue them in small claims court without having a lawyer. These are pretty much guaranteed wins for the consumers because you have proof on this date you mailed your letter and the credit bureau violated the law. You can get up to $2,500 if you can prove your case.

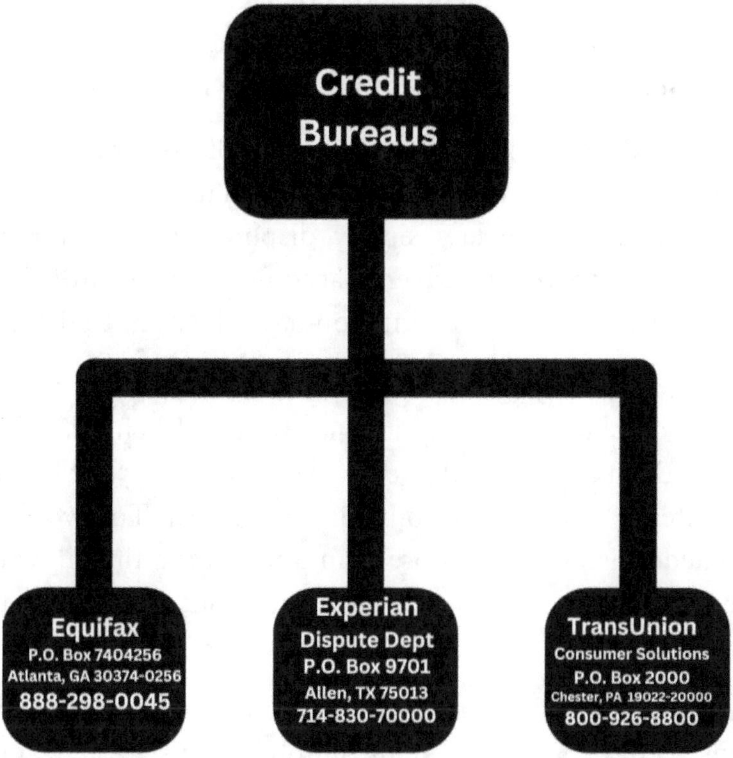

DISPUTING ADVERSE CREDIT ENTRIES

I want to clarify that I am not making a judgment on whether the adverse information on your credit report is true or false. Just like in a court of law, your lawyer would argue that you are innocent regardless of the circumstances. In the same way, I am here to support you and act as your advocate.

Throughout this book, I will encourage you to challenge any negative entries on your credit report. There may be mitigating evidence that supports your claim or perhaps the collection accounts or late payments do not actually belong to you. Additionally, it's possible that the statute of limitations has expired, making it illegal for the account to be reported.

It's prudent to note that Section 609 of the Fair Credit Reporting Act (FCRA) does not differentiate between valid and invalid accounts. The law simply disputes the credit reporting agency's right to report adverse accounts. So, regardless of the validity of the negative account, you have the right to dispute it.

When challenging information on your credit report, it's essential to follow certain guidelines to avoid being labeled as a frivolous disputer. This label can seriously harm your chances of getting items removed from your credit file. To avoid this, I recommend disputing no more than 5 items at a time in your 609 dispute letter and not disputing a particular item more than 4 times.

It's important to remember that the law doesn't allow you to dispute accurate negative items simply because you want them removed from your credit report. Late payments, debt, bankruptcy, collections, foreclosure, and other financial hardships will reflect on your credit report because they did happen. Therefore, it's a smart move to be careful not to be labeled as a frivolous dispute by the credit bureaus.

I strongly advise disputing an item only three times, which means sending a maximum of two follow-up letters after your initial dispute letter. If your dispute is not successful, the final step is to file a consumer complaint with the Consumer Financial Protection Bureau (CFPB) for review. Remember to follow these steps carefully to increase your chances of successfully disputing negative items on your credit report.

In any event, it is your right under the FCRA to challenge all inaccuracies in your credit report. Even the Federal Trade

Commission (FTC) states on their website that you should dispute EVERY item you think is not accurate, incomplete or unverifiable on your credit report in writing and by Certified Mail "return receipt requested". So once again, dispute everything. The great thing about this country is that there are loopholes. What that means is that even though you know the item is true, it can happen that the information was not reported correctly. Hence, you have a great argument for the item to be removed. I'm sure you heard of many guilty parties that got off on technicalities. I am advocating for finding any way possible to challenge any and all adverse information on your file. At the very least, send out a documentation/verification request to the credit bureaus. That is within your rights as a consumer under the FCRA.

You are entitled under the law to Dispute with the credit bureaus and Dispute directly with the collection agency or original creditor. We will begin our journey by disputing directly with the credit bureaus. I do not recommend disputing online with the credit bureaus. Disputing in writing contains much more benefits than online. For best result, I have included 4 secret letters that you can use to increase your odds of success. I recommend that you modify the letter slightly as a way to customize it based on your particular situation. Also, it's a good idea to customize as a way not to get "flagged" as a frivolous letter with the credit bureaus.

THE SECRET CREDIT DISPUTE LETTERS

1st letter: The Fair Credit Reporting Act (FCRA) section 611 allows for consumers to challenge questionable items on their credit reports. So you have a right to dispute information that you believe to be incorrect. This includes questionable late payments, collections, charge offs, tax liens, bankruptcies, judgments, foreclosures, or any personal identification information. The law allows basically any "questionable" negative or inaccurate information on your credit file can be disputed and their deletion may result in a credit score increase.

There are a few ways to dispute an item on your credit report including mailing a letter to the credit bureaus. Your credit dispute letter doesn't have to be fancy and it certainly doesn't have to come from a law firm. Your credit dispute should detail the error you found to be untrue and should be investigated. Your letter should also include supporting documents if available to help the bureaus conduct a proper investigation.

Disputing your credit report helps prevent dips to your overall credit score that could have a negative financial consequence on you including higher interest rates on loans or credit cards or being denied credit altogether.

I have included a template to be used to dispute your credit report. You can use this template or version of it to request that the information on your credit report is inaccurate and should be investigated. The preferred outcome of course is for the item to be removed from your credit report. You will print many copies of this 1st letter and then you will write the missing information with a pen. I found out this letter is very effective as an initial letter to challenge negative entries on your credit report and it can be used for all the 3 major credit bureaus.

This is the initial letter. Your aim is for the credit bureau to verify the account. In some cases, the account will not be verified (maybe because of the credit freeze) and the information is deleted. Great job. Pat yourself on the back for a job well done. However, most of the time, you will need to write more than one letter to succeed. That's ok because I have included all the follow up letters you would need to try to win your case.

<u>Sample letter #1</u> – Please customize your letter for fear that the Credit Bureaus may label your letter as "Frivolous" in which case the CRA can legally terminate a re-investigation of the information disputed by you. So try to change the letter a little for best results.

Credit Bureau Name:

____

Consumer ID/ Report #

____

Your name:

____

Today's date:

____

To Whom It May Concern:

I am writing to dispute that derogatory information from my account is falsely listed on my credit report with your bureau. I am requesting the account information to be properly verified as per FCRA. Lastly, the amount owed for the following account is no longer outstanding:

Company Name:

____

Original Creditor:

____

Original A/C #:

____

Amount: $

____

Reason(s) for Dispute:

- o This is not my account
- o I have never made a late payment
- o This account is more than seven (7) years old
- o This account is bankruptcy
- o This account is closed
- o I have paid this account in full
- o I paid this before it went to collections/charge-off
- o Other:

____

This is my official request to have the listed account investigated and removed from my credit report as this item is not accurate.

Enclosed may be additional evidence to support my claim.

Sincerely,

*Jane Doe

____

* Do not wet sign your signature as this may be used to verify an account.

All communications with the bureaus will be done via USPS Certified Mail.

Be sure to always include the following documents to establish your identity and place of residence of all communications with the credit bureaus:

- Copy of the credit report section in question
- Copy of driver license or Non-Driver license
- Utility bill: gas or electric....
- S.S. card
- Supporting documentation supporting your claim like a deletion from the creditor

---

****** wait for 30 days for the outcome. If not happy with the outcome, then go to letter #2

***** If the creditor fails to verify your disputed account within thirty(30) days then they must delete it.

***** Always keep track of the clock. Make sure to document everything in case you have to complaint/sue the credit bureau

---

Before we move on to the 2nd letter to the credit bureau, I want you to write a letter to the original creditor as part of the dispute process. That way, you will cover all bases.

Sample letter:

Company Name:

____

Collection A/C#:

____

Your name:

____

Today's Date:

____

Dear Collector,

I am writing to dispute the following information that your company supplied to __________________________. I do not believe that I owe this debt or the amount stated on my credit report.

I respectfully request the following:

1- The total amount of the debt

2- The legal owner of this alleged debt

3- Please include original purchase agreement -terms and conditions of the debt

4- The name of the creditor to whom the debt is owed

5- Verification or copy of any judgment

Please take notice that I have disputed this debt. Therefore, until it is validated, your information concerning this debt is assumed to be inaccurate. Kindly inform the credit bureau of my dispute with this debt. Reporting information that you know to be inaccurate or failing to report information correctly violates the Fair Credit Reporting Act S 1681s-2.

Should you continue on your path without validating this debt, I will inform the judge and request that the case be dismissed based on your failure to comply with the FDCPA.

Sincerely,

Jane Doe

All communications with the creditor will be done via USPS Certified Mail.

2nd letter: Validation or Method of Verification. Once your debt has been verified by the creditor immediately request for Validation which means prove it to me in writing. Validation is more legally binding. The next letter will request under Section 609 of the FCRA, that the CRA send you a copy of the original contract that you signed – that they are supposed to have. NEVER pay any debt without Valid proof. It's the law.

If the account is being verified which means to confirm or substantiate in law by oath- then, they by law, are supposed to have a copy of the contract to do so or provide a method of legally verifying the account. Since they will not be able to provide the contract you signed most of the time, then by law, the derogatory information must be deleted.

Please be aware that under the FCRA law, the CRA's must provide you a copy of the signed contract if you request it. Since most of the time, they will be unable to provide you a copy, then the account will be UNVERIFIED and under the Federal Law any UNVERIFIED accounts must be deleted.

I'm assuming that the 1st letter came back as "verified" and nothing has changed on your credit report so far. Now that the disputed item was not deleted and most likely came back as verified; I want you to send out a follow up letter to the credit bureau. This time you will not ask for the item to be deleted but you will ask the item to be validated in the form of a validation letter. Also, you will request a method of verification that they used to authenticate the account. See sample letter below.

Sample letter #2 - Please customize your letter for fear that the Credit Bureaus may label your letter as "Frivolous" in which case the CRA can legally terminate a re-investigation of the information disputed by you. So try to change the letter a little for best results.

Credit Bureau Name:

____

Consumer ID/ Report #

____

Your name:

____

Today's Date:

____

To Whom It May Concern:

This is a follow up letter to the original dispute letter sent on __________ . Please see attached. This account is still inaccurate and your company is still continuing to report derogatory marks on my credit file, which is adversely affecting my credit score and my ability to obtain credit. Credit reporting laws ensure that bureaus report only 100% accurate credit information.

Every step must be taken to assure the information reported is completely accurate and correct. The following information, therefore, needs to be re-investigated. Please make sure everything pertaining to my credit report is correct.

Please be advised that I have requested the debt collector/creditor inform you that I am disputed about this pending debt validation.

Account Name:

____

Account Number:

____

I am requesting that the information on my credit file be validated as per rules set forth under the FCRA. Please provide me with the following items in regards to this account:

- Contract with my signature
- Legal owner of alleged debt
- Credit Insurance
- Interest Rate Disclosure
- Payment History Balance History
- Balance History

I respectfully ask for this credit bureau to provide some kind of proof of this alleged item, specifically the contract, note, or other instrument bearing my signature.

Additionally, please provide the name, address, and telephone number of each credit grantor or other subscriber.

I also heard that under federal law, you have thirty (30) days to complete your re-investigation. Be advised that the description of the procedure used to determine the accuracy and completeness of the information is hereby requested as well, to be provided within fifteen (15) days of the completion of your re-investigation.

Sincerely,

*Jane Doe

A 2nd letter should also be sent to the creditor as part of the dispute process.

Sample letter #2(a)

Credit Bureau Name: ____________________

Consumer ID/ Report # ____________________

Your name: ____________________

Today's Date: ____________________

To Whom It May Concern:

This is a follow up letter to the original dispute letter sent on ____________ . Please see attached. This account is still inaccurate and your company is still continuing to report derogatory marks on my credit file, which is adversely affecting my credit score and my ability to obtain credit. Credit reporting laws ensure that bureaus report only 100% accurate credit information. Every step must be taken to assure the information reported is completely accurate and correct. The following information, therefore, needs to be re-investigated. Please make sure everything pertaining to my credit report is correct.

Please be advised that I have requested the debt collector/creditor inform you that I am disputed this pending debt validation.

Account Name: ________________________________

Account Number: ________________________________

Account Name: ________________________________

Account Number: ________________________________

Account Name: ________________________________

Account Number: ________________________________

Account Name: ________________________________

Account Number: ________________________________

I am requesting that the information on my credit file be validated as per rules set forth under the FCRA. Please provide me with the following items in regards to this account:

- Contract with my signature
- Pay Off disclosure
- Credit Insurance
- Interest Rate Disclosure
- Payment History Balance History
- Balance History

I respectfully ask for this credit bureau to provide some kind of proof of this alleged item, specifically the contract, note, or other instrument bearing my signature.

Additionally, please provide the name, address, and telephone number of each credit grantor or other subscriber.

I also heard that under federal law, you have thirty (30) days to complete your re-investigation. Be advised that the description of the procedure used to determine the accuracy and completeness of the information is hereby requested as well, to be provided within fifteen (15) days of the completion of your re-investigation.

Sincerely,

*Jane Doe

---

* Do not wet sign your signature as this may be used to verify an account. – Only sign if you have to notarize your letter.

All communications with the bureaus will be done via USPS Certified Mail.

Be sure to always include the following documents to establish your identity and place of residence of all communications with the credit bureaus:

- Copy of the credit report section in question
- Copy of the 1st dispute letter
- Copy of driver license or Non-Driver license
- Utility bill: gas or electric....
- S.S. card
- Supporting documentation supporting your claim like a deletion from a creditor

---

****** wait for 30 days for the outcome. If not happy with the outcome, then go to letter #3

***** If the creditor fails to verify your disputed account within thirty(30) days then they must delete it.

***** Always keep track of the clock. Make sure to document everything in case you have to complaint/sue the credit bureau

---

When you send your letters to the credit bureaus, it is quite possible that they might try to ignore you and hope that you will just go away. Do not fall victim to the credit bureaus' tactics. From experience, the credit bureau might send you a reply saying a "suspicious letter" was sent on your behalf but has been set aside. This is done to intimidate you to stop continuing disputing the item(s). Do not fall for it. Stay vigilante.

Here are some common responses to discourage you from further disputing "We received a suspicious request regarding your personal credit information that we have determined was not sent by you. We have not taken any action on this request and any future requests made in this manner will not be processed and will not receive a response".

Another likely response from the credit bureau might be: "Suspicious requests are taken seriously and reviewed by security personnel who will report deceptive activity, including copies of letters deemed as suspicious, to law enforcement officials and to state or federal regulatory agencies".

Credit bureaus also can ask for proof of your identity and request you mail them. If this happens, notarize* your next letter along with the aforementioned list of supporting documents. Now you have no choice but to sign your letters going forward.

*Sent a notarized letter identification form with the following verbiage: "I declare under penalty of perjury (under the laws of the United States of America) that this identification is provided by me".

3rd letter - I'm assuming that the 2nd letter came back as "verified" and nothing has changed on your credit report so far. We will then go on to the next letter. Don't be discouraged. This is a marathon, not a sprint. We have to stay the course. Now we will try another method. This time you will state that the account was not properly verified and that the credit bureau is violating your rights of privacy. See sample letter below.

<u>Sample letter #3</u>- Please customize your letter for fear that the Credit Bureaus may label your letter as "Frivolous" in which case the CRA can legally terminate a re-investigation of the information disputed by you. So try to change the letter a little for best results.

Credit Bureau Name: ______________________

Consumer ID/ Report # ______________________

Your name: ______________________

Today's Date: ______________________

To Whom It May Concern:

I recently sent you a request on ________________ and ________________ to investigate and re-investigate inaccurate information reported to the credit agencies. As a consumer, I am very aware of all my rights under the law which are protected by the Congress under the Fair Credit Reporting Act (FCRA). The list of accounts below has violated my federally protected consumer rights to privacy and confidentiality under 15 USC 1681.

Account Name: ________________________________

Account Name: ________________________________

- 15 U.S.C. 1681 Section 602 A. States I have the right to privacy
- 15 U.S.C. 1681 Section 604 A Section 2: States a consumer reporting agency cannot furnish an account without my written instructions

I demand this account be deleted immediately as I did not give anyone written instructions. You also failed to provide the requested documentation to validate the disputed account nor provided the method of verification. Furthermore, the collection company/creditor also failed to validate the debt. I remind you that under the FCRA, unverified accounts must be removed from my credit report.

Please remove this item from my credit report or your company will be in violation of the FCRA. If not removed, I will then escalate this matter by filing a complaint with the Consumer Financial Protection Bureau (CFPB) or Office of the General Attorney.

Please note that I have opted out in writing to your forced arbitration terms and am willing to seek legal relief in accordance with the FCRA.

Sincerely,

*Jane Doe

Sample letter #3(a)

Credit Bureau Name:

____

Consumer ID/ Report #

____

Your name:

____

Today's Date:

____

To Whom It May Concern:

I recently sent you a request on ____________________ and __________________ to investigate and re-investigate inaccurate information reported to the credit agencies. As a consumer, I am very aware of all my rights under the law which are protected by the Congress under the Fair Credit Reporting Act (FCRA). The list of accounts below has violated my federally protected consumer rights to privacy and confidentiality under 15 USC 1681.

Account Name: ______________________________

Account Number: ______________________________

Account Name: ______________________________

Account Number: ______________________________

Account Name: ______________________________

Account Number: ______________________________

Account Name: ______________________________

Account Number: ______________________________

- 15 U.S.C. 1681 Section 602 A. States I have the right to privacy
- 15 U.S.C. 1681 Section 604 A Section 2: States a consumer reporting agency cannot furnish an account without my written instructions

I demand this account be deleted immediately as I did not give anyone written instructions. You also failed to provide the requested documentation to validate the disputed account nor provided the method of verification. Furthermore, the collection company/creditor also failed to validate the debt. I remind you that under the FCRA, unverified accounts must be removed from my credit report.

Please remove this item from my credit report or your company will be in violation of the FCRA. If not removed, I will then escalate this matter by filing a complaint with the Consumer Financial Protection Bureau (CFPB) or Office of the General Attorney.

Please note that I have opted out in writing to your forced arbitration terms and am willing to seek legal relief in accordance with the FCRA.

Sincerely,

*Jane Doe

---

* Do not wet sign your signature as this may be used to verify an account. – Only sign if you have to notarize your letter.

All communications with the bureaus will be done via USPS Certified Mail.

Be sure to always include the following documents to establish your identity and place of residence of all communications with the credit bureaus:

- Copy of the credit report section in question
- Copy of the 1st and 2nd dispute letter

- Copy of driver license or Non-Driver license
- Utility bill: gas or electric....
- S.S. card
- Documentation supporting your claim like a deletion letter from the creditor

---

***** wait for 30 days for the outcome. If not happy with the outcome, then go to letter #4

***** If the creditor fails to verify your disputed account within thirty(30) days then they must delete it.

***** Always keep track of the clock. Make sure to document everything in case you have to complaint/sue the credit bureau

---

When you send your letters to the credit bureaus, it is quite possible that they might try to ignore you and hope that you will just go away. Do not fall victim to the credit bureaus. From experience, the credit bureau might send you a reply saying a "suspicious letter" was sent on your behalf but has been set aside. This is done to intimidate you to stop continuing disputing the item(s). Do not fall for it. Stay vigilante.

Here are some common responses to discourage you from further disputing "We received a suspicious request regarding your personal credit information that we have determined was not sent by you. We have not taken any action on this request and any future requests made in this manner will not be processed and will not receive a response".

Another likely response from the credit bureau might be: "Suspicious requests are taken seriously and reviewed by security personnel who will report deceptive activity, including copies of letters deemed as suspicious, to law enforcement officials and to state or federal regulatory agencies".

Credit bureaus also can ask for proof of your identity and request you mail them. If this happens, notarize* your next letter along with the aforementioned list of supporting documents. Now you have no choice but to sign your letters going forward.

*Sent a notarized letter identification form with the following verbiage: "I declare under penalty of perjury (under the laws of the United States of America) that this identification is provided by me".

4th Letter – This is the Final Letter you will send to the credit bureau before you escalate this matter by filing a complaint with the CFPB. Also, you can file a complaint with the Attorney General in your state. This is not the time to retreat but to resurgence. You have made it this far. I am very proud of you. However, the job is still not done. You still need to delete these accounts from your credit report. Green pasture awaits you in the form of good credit. So let us continue doing the hard work. I promise you it will be worth it.

Do not be discouraged as you have a lot of tools available to you. Like I said before, you can file a complaint with the CFPB where the credit bureau can be sanctioned or you can file a complaint with the Attorney General in your state. You also have the option of suing the credit bureau in small claim court. You can hire a lawyer specializing in suing credit bureaus where he/she can file the complaint and you can be awarded up to $1,000 in monetary damages for each violation of the FCRA. The credit bureau can also be liable for attorney fees. You can do a search on google for lawyers that sue credit bureaus.

Sample letter #4- Please customize your letter for fear that the Credit Bureaus may label your letter as "Frivolous" in which case the CRA can legally terminate a re-investigation of the information disputed by you. So try to change the letter a little for best results.

Credit Bureau Name:

____

Consumer ID/ Report #

____

Your name:

____

Today's Date:

____

To Whom It May Concern:

Please be advised that this is my FOURTH WRITTEN REQUEST and FINAL WARNING that I fully intend to pursue litigation in accordance with the FCRA to enforce my rights and seek relief and recover all monetary damages under Section 616 and Section 617 regarding your continued willful and negligent noncompliance.

I recently sent you a request on ________________, ________________ and ________________ to investigate and re-investigate inaccurate information reported to the credit agencies.

Account Name:

____

Account Number:

____

In the results of your initial investigation and subsequent reinvestigations, you stated that you "verified" that these items are being "reported correctly". I'm still in doubt as to how the account was verified? You have yet to provide a copy of any original documentation with my signature on it as required according to Section 609(a)(1)(A) & Section 611(a)(1)(A).

Furthermore, I have not satisfactorily received the method of verification as required under section 611(a)(7).

I remind you under Section 611 (5)(A) of the FCRA, you are required to "…. Promptly DELETE all information which cannot be verified.

The law is crystal clear as to the Civil Liability and the remedy available to me (Section 616 & 617) if you repeatedly failed to comply with Federal Laws. I have been negatively impacted by your continued failure to delete UNVERIFIED accounts.

Please note that I have opted out in writing to your forced arbitration terms. I fully intend on pursuing litigation in this matter to enforce my rights under the FCRA.

Sincerely,

*Jane Doe

Sample letter #4(a)

Credit Bureau Name:

____

Consumer ID/ Report #

____

Your name:

____

Today's Date:

____

To Whom It May Concern:

Please be advised that this is my FOURTH WRITTEN REQUEST and FINAL WARNING that I fully intend to pursue litigation in accordance with the FCRA to enforce my rights and seek relief and recover all monetary damages under Section 616 and Section 617 regarding your continued willful and negligent noncompliance.

I recently sent you a request on ________________ , ________________ and ________________ to investigate and re-investigate inaccurate information reported to the credit agencies.

Account Name: ______________________________

Account Number: ______________________________

Account Name: ______________________________

Account Number: ______________________________

Account Name: ______________________________

Account Number: ______________________________

Account Name: ______________________________

Account Number: ______________________________

In the results of your initial investigation and subsequent reinvestigations, you stated that you "verified" that these items are being "reported correctly". I'm still in doubt as to how the account was verified? You have yet to provide a copy of any original documentation with my signature on it as required Section 609(a)(1)(A) & Section 611(a)(1)(A).

Furthermore, I have not satisfactorily received the method of verification as required under section 611(a)(7).

I remind you under Section 611 (5)(A) of the FCRA, you are required to ".... Promptly DELETE all information which cannot be verified.

The law is crystal clear as to the Civil Liability and the remedy available to me (Section 616 & 617) if you repeatedly failed to comply with Federal Laws. I have been negatively impacted by your continued failure to delete UNVERIFIED accounts.

Please note that I have opted out in writing to your forced arbitration terms. I fully intend on pursuing litigation in this matter to enforce my rights under the FCRA.

Sincerely,

*Jane Doe

---

* Do not wet sign your signature as this may be used to verify an account. – Only sign if you have to notarize your letter.

All communications with the bureaus will be done via USPS Certified Mail.

Be sure to always include the following documents to establish your identity and place of residence of all communications with the credit bureaus:

- Copy of the credit report section in question
- Copy of the 1st and 2nd dispute letter

- Copy of driver license or Non-Driver license
- Utility bill: gas or electric....
- S.S. card
- Supporting documentation supporting your claim like a deletion letter from the creditor

---

***** wait for 30 days for the outcome. If not happy with the outcome, then proceed to file a complaint and you can exercise your rights to sue the credit bureau

***** If the creditor fails to verify your disputed account within thirty(30) days then they must delete it.

***** Always keep track of the clock. Make sure to document everything in case you have to complaint/sue the credit bureau

---

COMPLAINING TO THE CFPB

We have exhausted all means to resolve this conflict amicably; however, we have no choice but to file a complaint. It is time to file a federal complaint with the Consumer Protection Bureau (CFPB). Remember that there are important consumer rights guaranteed by the federal consumer financial law. After you spent all these times by writing letter after letter to resolve this matter with the CRA, it is now time to change course. Remember protecting your federally protected rights is paramount. Do not let the credit bureaus take your rights away.

The complaint process is not as complicated as you might think. It's just a matter of going on the website and answering pertinent questions. Also, you would need to upload all your correspondences from and to the credit bureau that supports your case. The CFPB is available to assist you with the following:

- Incorrect information on a credit report
- A Consumer reporting agency's investigation

- The improper use of a credit report
- Unable to get credit report or credit score
- Issues with credit monitoring or identify protection services

Furthermore, the CFPB has expanded to handle complaints ranging from credit cards, complaints on mortgages, bank accounts and services, consumer loans, and private student loans.

You are given a tracking number after submitting a complaint with the CFPB which allows you to check the status of the complaint periodically by logging on to the CFPB website. The CFPB complaint is processed case by case and sent to the company for response. The rule set forth by CFPB is for the company to provide a response within 15 days with the steps they have taken or plan on taking. Also, within the rules set forth by CFPB, a consumer will have the option to dispute the company's response to the complaint.

You have come from a long way; stopping now is not an option. You have spent your money buying this book. You have taken the time to read this book and you have implemented all the steps outlined in this book to remove derogatory marks on your credit report. But so far, you have not gotten the perfect results that you were hoping for. Maybe you are able to remove 1 or 2 items. Maybe you have removed most items. But there's a few adverse marks lingering on your credit file that the credit bureau or the creditor refused to remove. Do not despair. Good credit score awaits.

A central part of the CFPB mission is to stand up for consumers and make sure they are treated fairly in the financial marketplace. CFPB is authorized to conduct investigations to determine whether any person is, or has, engaged in conduct that violates Federal Consumer Financial Law. CFPB has the authority to hold financial service providers accountable for their actions.

The CFPB may impose sanctions or other public enforcement actions on the financial companies.

The website for the CFPB is: https://www.consumerfinance.gov/complaint/ or you can call them at (855) 411-2372.

The main complaint will be as follows: "I sent the credit bureaus letters asking them to verify the debt on my report. The credit bureau sent it back as "verified" with no supporting documents. I subsequently asked the credit bureau to provide a method of verification which I have not received. My credit report is still showing inaccuracies. 15 U.S>C. 1681s-2(A)(1) states a person shall not furnish any information relating to a consumer to any consumer reporting agency if the person knows or has reasonable cause to believe that the information is inaccurate.

Under the heading "what would be a fair resolution to this issue", I want you to state "I want the item(s) removed from my credit report immediately".

SUING THE CREDIT BUREAU

In accordance with the Fair Credit Reporting Act (FCRA), you have a right to the fair and accurate reporting of your credit information. FCRA also grants you certain privacy rights concerning your credit information and protection from the misuse of your credit report. When your rights are violated under the FCRA, you have some remedies available. Those remedies might include actual damages, punitive damages, attorneys' fees, and costs. The type of remedy available will depend on whether the violation was intentional or negligent.

Since I have to give you the good and bad. You should be aware of the penalty for a Frivolous FCRA lawsuit. The FCRA has a penalty for filing a lawsuit or subsequent court papers that are later determined to have been filed in “bad faith or for purposes of harassment”. The defendant in this case might have to pay the other side’s attorney fees if it was determined you file bad faith papers and lose. (15 U.S.C. S 1681n.15 U.S.C. S 1681o).

If you determined on your volition that the best course of action is to sue the credit bureau, you can file a complaint in either federal court or your state’s court, subject to statute of limitations. In most states, you must file your complaint 2 years after the date you discovered the violation or 5 years after the date of the violation (15 U.S.C.A. S 1681p). You can file the complaint by yourself (on your own behalf) or you can hire a lawyer.

TIP ON HOW TO REMOVE HARD INQUIRIES FROM YOUR CREDIT REPORT

If you have hard inquiries on your credit report, there are several steps you can take to try to remove them. First, you can try to dispute the inquiry with the credit bureau. This involves sending a written dispute letter to the credit bureau, along with any supporting documentation, requesting that they remove the inquiry from your report. The credit bureau has 30 days to investigate the dispute and respond to you with their findings. If they determine that the inquiry was not authorized, they will remove it from your report

Another option is to contact the creditor who made the inquiry and request that they remove it from your report. You can do this by sending a goodwill letter, which is a written request asking the creditor to remove the inquiry as a gesture of goodwill. This approach is more likely to be successful if you have a good relationship with the creditor or if the inquiry was made in error.

You can also try to remove hard inquiries by using credit monitoring services or credit repair companies. These services can help you identify any errors or unauthorized inquiries on your report and dispute them on your behalf. However, it's fundamental to do your research and choose a reputable service or company to ensure that you don't fall victim to credit repair scams.

Lastly, it is significant to note that hard inquiries will typically remain on your credit report for two years. However, their impact on your credit score will decrease over time, and after a year or so, they will have a minimal effect on your credit score. By taking these steps to remove hard inquiries, you can improve your credit score and increase your chances of being approved for credit in the future.

SOFT INQUIRY EXPLAINS

A soft inquiry, also known as a soft pull, is a type of credit inquiry that does not affect your credit score. Unlike hard inquiries, soft inquiries are not visible to lenders and do not appear on your credit report that's available to them. Examples of soft inquiries include pre-approval offers, background checks, and checking your own credit score. Soft inquiries can also be made by lenders or credit card companies for the purpose of offering you promotional offers or increasing your credit limit. While soft inquiries do not have a negative impact on your credit, it's still important to monitor them to ensure that they are not a result of identity theft or fraud. It's also important to note that while soft inquiries do not affect your credit score, they can still appear on your personal credit report that you have access to.

Taking everything into consideration, keeping track of both hard and soft inquiries on your credit report is paramount to maintaining good credit health. While hard inquiries can have a negative impact on your credit score, taking steps to remove them and being mindful of when they occur can help mitigate their effects. On the other hand, regularly checking your credit score and report for any soft inquiries, as well as having a security freeze in place, can help protect you against identity theft and fraud. By being proactive and staying informed about your credit, you can work towards building and maintaining a healthy credit profile.

CONCLUSION

I have provided a comprehensive guide on how to remove derogatory marks from your credit report and covered the important role that the FCRA plays in consumer credit reporting. However, it's important to note that each individual case is unique and I cannot guarantee that all of the methods mentioned in this book will work. I simply aim to share my knowledge of credit repair with those who need it most. As a resident of New York, I am passionate about ensuring that Americans have access to the information they need to improve their credit and succeed in society. Bad credit can be very costly, and my goal is to empower average Americans to take control of their credit and improve their financial futures. This information should not be taken as an endorsement or opposition to bankruptcy, as every individual must make their own decision based on their unique circumstances.

My goal in sharing credit repair tactics is not to put credit repair companies out of business, but to empower individuals with knowledge on how to improve their credit. While I cannot guarantee the success of these tactics in your specific circumstances, I can assure you that credit repair companies use similar methods daily. However, unlike credit repair companies that charge monthly subscription fees without clear explanations of their actions, I am providing you with comprehensive information on how to navigate the credit bureaus and improve your credit on your own.

Credit repair can seem daunting, but it doesn't have to be. By purchasing this book, you have taken the first step toward repairing your credit. Now, it's time to implement the strategies outlined in the book and take control of your financial future.

Please be aware that credit repair is not a simple process and may require individualized assistance. If you have particular concerns or need support with a specific issue, feel free to contact me at Powerofcredit@gmail.com for personalized guidance.

BONUS BOOK:

BANKRUPTCY

FINANCIAL STRESS

THE DECISION

THE DECISION: The decision to file for bankruptcy can feel overwhelming and seems like the end of the world. But it's indispensable to remember that many successful individuals have faced financial hardship and come out on top. Just look at famous figures like Abraham Lincoln, Walt Disney, and Henry Ford. All of them have filed for bankruptcy at some point in their lives, yet they went on to achieve great success in their respective fields.

Abraham Lincoln, our 16th President, was a successful lawyer and politician before he fell on hard times. In 1833, he opened a general store in Illinois with a partner. Unfortunately, the business struggled and accumulated large debts. Lincoln took responsibility for the debts and eventually filed for bankruptcy, which at the time was a difficult and public process. However, he continued to work hard and eventually became one of the most revered leaders in American history.

Similarly, Walt Disney faced financial ruin in the early years of his animation studio. After losing the rights to his popular Oswald the Lucky Rabbit character, Disney struggled to keep his company afloat. In 1923, he filed for bankruptcy and began working on a new character, Mickey Mouse. The rest, as they say, is history. Disney went on to build an entertainment empire that still dominates the industry today.

Even Henry Ford, founder of Ford Motor Company and one of the most successful businessmen in history, faced bankruptcy early on in his career. In 1901, Ford founded the Detroit Automobile Company, which failed after just one year. He went on to start two more unsuccessful automobile companies before finally founding the Ford Motor Company in 1903.

These stories of resilience and success in the face of bankruptcy serve as powerful reminders that financial hardships can happen to anyone. The key is to stay focused, work hard, and never give up. With determination and the right support, it is possible to bounce back from even the toughest financial setbacks.

WHAT IS BANKRUPTCY

Bankruptcy is a statutory process that provides individuals and businesses with a way to deal with overwhelming debt. There are several chapters of bankruptcy under the United States Bankruptcy Code, each with its own set of rules and requirements.

Chapter 7 bankruptcy is the most common form of bankruptcy and is often referred to as a "liquidation bankruptcy." In Chapter 7, a court-appointed trustee sells the debtor's non-exempt assets to pay off creditors. Any remaining debts are then discharged, meaning the debtor is no longer responsible for paying them.

Famous examples of actors who filed for Chapter 7 bankruptcy include Burt Reynolds, Gary Busey, and MC Hammer. In 2012, singer Toni Braxton also filed for Chapter 7 bankruptcy due to debts from health issues and bad contracts.

Chapter 11 bankruptcy is a reorganization bankruptcy often used by businesses. It allows a business to continue operating while it reorganizes its finances and debt obligations. The debtor creates a reorganization plan that outlines how it will pay off creditors[8] over time.

[8] In a Chapter 11 bankruptcy, there are two types of debtors: first position and secondary position. First position debtors are creditors who have priority in receiving payment from the debtor's assets. These creditors usually consist of secured creditors who hold a lien on the debtor's property or assets, such as a mortgage lender or equipment lessor. They are given priority because their debts are secured by the debtor's assets, which means that they have a legal claim on them in the event of default.

Famous examples of musicians who filed for Chapter 11 bankruptcy include 50 Cent, who filed in 2015 due to a failed business venture, and the rock band Guns N' Roses, who filed in 2009 to reorganize their finances and negotiate contracts.

Chapter 13 bankruptcy is a type of reorganization bankruptcy for individuals with a steady income. In Chapter 13, the debtor creates a repayment plan to pay off creditors over three to five years.

Famous examples of actors who filed for Chapter 13 bankruptcy include Stephen Baldwin, who filed in 2009 due to a mortgage on his home, and Gary Coleman, who filed in 1999 due to medical bills and legal fees.

THE US BANKRUPTCY CODE

The US Bankruptcy Code is a federal law that outlines the procedures and requirements for individuals and businesses to file for bankruptcy protection. It was first enacted in 1978 and has since undergone several amendments to address various economic and social changes.

The Code is divided into several chapters, each of which outlines a different type of bankruptcy filing. Chapter 7 bankruptcy involves liquidation of assets to pay off creditors, while Chapter 13 bankruptcy involves a repayment plan for individuals.

On the other hand, secondary position debtors are those who do not have a priority claim on the debtor's assets. They are typically unsecured creditors, such as suppliers or vendors who have provided goods or services to the debtor but do not hold a security interest in the debtor's assets. These creditors are typically paid after the first position creditors are satisfied, which means that they may receive a lower amount or no payment at all depending on the debtor's assets and financial situation.

Chapter 11 bankruptcy is typically used by businesses and allows for reorganization of debt and continued operation.

The Code also establishes the role of bankruptcy courts and trustees, who oversee bankruptcy cases and make decisions regarding the distribution of assets and repayment plans. The Code also provides for certain exemptions, which allow individuals to protect certain assets from being liquidated in bankruptcy proceedings.

The US Bankruptcy Code has undergone several key amendments over time. Initially enacted in 1898, the Bankruptcy Act was designed to help businesses and individuals reorganize their finances and avoid complete financial ruin. It underwent significant revisions in 1938 and again in 1978, with the latter replacing the previous act entirely.

The 1978 Bankruptcy Code included several chapters, including Chapter 7, Chapter 11, Chapter 12, and Chapter 13. Chapter 7 provides for the liquidation of assets in order to pay off creditors, while Chapter 11 allows businesses to reorganize and continue operating. Chapter 12 is specific to farmers and fishermen, and Chapter 13 provides for a repayment plan for individuals with regular income.

The Bankruptcy Abuse Prevention and Consumer Protection Act (BAPCPA) of 2005 was another significant amendment to the Bankruptcy Code. It was designed to make it more difficult for individuals to file for Chapter 7 bankruptcy and instead encourage them to file for Chapter 13, which requires a repayment plan. It also introduced a means test to determine eligibility for Chapter 7 bankruptcy and increased the requirements for credit counseling.

Overall, the US Bankruptcy Code is designed to provide relief for individuals and businesses struggling with overwhelming debt, while also balancing the rights of creditors to receive repayment for debts owed to them. If you are currently experiencing financial difficulties, it's crucial to keep in mind that the Bankruptcy Code can provide protections to help you reorganize your finances and move forward. With the help of an experienced bankruptcy attorney, you can explore the different options available under the code and determine the best path forward for your specific situation. Remember, you are not alone and there are resources available to help you regain financial stability.

THE BANKRUPTCY PROCESS

Bankruptcy is a lawful procedure that grants individuals and businesses the opportunity to restructure or discharge some or all of their debts. The procedure is regulated by the Bankruptcy Code, a federal law, and is adjudicated in federal bankruptcy courts. The fundamental objective of bankruptcy is to provide the debtor with a new beginning by reorganizing or discharging their debts. It offers a way for individuals who are burdened by debt to have a fresh start and regain control of their finances. Here are the standard procedures for a bankruptcy case:

When an individual or business decides to file for bankruptcy, they must provide full disclosure of their assets, liabilities, income, and expenses to the court. The type of bankruptcy they file will determine which assets are exempt from creditors. After filing the bankruptcy petition, an automatic stay is put in place, which stops creditors from taking any action against the debtor's assets or attempting to collect debts.

As mentioned earlier, bankruptcy is not a one-size-fits-all solution, and there are different types of bankruptcy available depending on the individual or business's situation. The most common types of bankruptcy are Chapter 7, Chapter 11, and Chapter 13.

Chapter 7, also referred to as "straight bankruptcy[9]," involves the liquidation of assets to pay off creditors. This type of bankruptcy is generally seen as a last resort because it may result in the loss of assets to pay off debts.

Chapter 11 is typically used by businesses and involves the reorganization of the debtor's affairs under court supervision. The debtor can continue business operations while repaying their debts.

Chapter 13 is intended for individuals with regular income and involves a repayment plan over a period of three to five years. This type of bankruptcy is often the best option for those who want to keep their assets and repay their debts over time.

Over the years, the bankruptcy code has undergone several amendments to better protect debtors' rights and simplify the process. These changes include the Bankruptcy Abuse Prevention and Consumer Protection Act of 2005, which added stricter requirements for individuals filing for bankruptcy, and the Small Business Reorganization Act of 2019, which made it easier for small businesses to restructure their debts.

Understanding that the bankruptcy process is complex and intricate is crucial, as it comes with significant long-term consequences. Therefore, it is highly recommended that individuals consult with a bankruptcy attorney to determine whether bankruptcy is the right option for their situation, and to gain an understanding of the various types of bankruptcy that are available.

[9] The first recorded instance of straight bankruptcy, also known as Chapter 7 bankruptcy, was in England in the early 19th century. The concept was later adopted by the United States and included in the Bankruptcy Act of 1898.

One such type is Chapter 7 bankruptcy, which is commonly referred to as "liquidation" or "straight bankruptcy." This form of bankruptcy involves the liquidation of non-exempt assets belonging to the debtor, which are sold to pay off their creditors. Typically, individuals who do not possess the means to repay their debts and lack significant assets they wish to protect opt for Chapter 7 bankruptcy. The process of filing for Chapter 7 bankruptcy involves the submission of a petition to the bankruptcy court by the debtor, which includes a comprehensive list of their assets, liabilities, income, and expenses. Once the petition is approved, a trustee is appointed by the court to take control of the debtor's non-exempt assets and sell them off to repay creditors. Additionally, the debtor is required to attend a "341 meeting," during which they will be questioned under oath by the trustee and their creditors regarding their financial situation.

In order to qualify for Chapter 7 bankruptcy, the debtor must pass a means test and meet certain other requirements. If they do qualify, the court will typically discharge the debtor's unsecured debts such as credit card balances, medical bills, and personal loans. It should be highlighted that, however, that not all types of debt can be discharged in Chapter 7 bankruptcy. For example, student loans[10], taxes, and child support are generally not eligible for discharge. Additionally, some assets may not be protected and may be sold in order to pay off creditors, depending on the state laws and the debtor's circumstances.

Chapter 11 bankruptcy is a type of bankruptcy that is generally used by businesses seeking to restructure their finances and debt. Compared to other types of bankruptcy, it is more

[10] Discharging student loans through bankruptcy can be a challenging process. In order to do so, the borrower must file a separate lawsuit called an "adversary proceeding" in bankruptcy court and prove that repaying the loan would cause "undue hardship." This requires meeting a specific legal standard that is difficult to meet, and the borrower may need to hire an attorney to help them through the process. Overall, discharging student loans in bankruptcy is a complex and difficult process. Although there have been recent efforts to change the rules, as of now, discharging student loans through bankruptcy is not a viable option for many borrowers.

intricate and versatile as it permits the debtor to maintain control of their business operations and assets while creating a plan to repay their creditors.

Under Chapter 11, the debtor must file a petition with the bankruptcy court, which appoints a trustee to supervise the case. The debtor then prepares a plan of reorganization outlining how they will restructure their business, pay their debts, and recover their profitability. This plan must be approved by the court and by the creditors, who have the right to vote on the plan.

During the Chapter 11 process, the debtor retains control of their business and operations, but under the oversight of the court and trustee. This allows the debtor to continue generating revenue and maintaining their workforce. The debtor can reject unprofitable contracts, reduce their debts, and emerge with a stronger financial position after the process. However, it bears mentioning that Chapter 11 bankruptcy can be a prolonged and intricate process, and the filing and administration costs can be expensive. There is also no guarantee that the plan of reorganization will be approved, and the business may ultimately liquidate if an agreement cannot be reached.

Chapter 13 bankruptcy is designed for individuals with a regular income who want to repay some or all of their debts over a period of three to five years. To file for Chapter 13 bankruptcy, the debtor must submit a repayment plan to the court that outlines how they plan to repay their creditors. The debtor must make regular payments to a court-appointed trustee, who will distribute the funds to the creditors according to the repayment plan.

One significant advantage of Chapter 13 bankruptcy is that it allows debtors to keep their assets, such as their home or car, while they pay off their debts. This can be particularly helpful for individuals facing foreclosure or repossession of their property. Additionally, Chapter 13 bankruptcy can help debtors address both secured and unsecured debts. It can even allow the debtor to modify the terms of their secured debts to make them more affordable, reducing the amount they owe. It's vital to keep in mind that Chapter 13 bankruptcy is a long-term commitment and requires regular payments for the duration of the repayment plan. Also, less discharge of debt is provided compared to Chapter 7 bankruptcy. To determine whether Chapter 13 bankruptcy is the right option, it is advisable to consult with a bankruptcy attorney who can evaluate your income, expenses, and total amount of debt owed.

WHAT ARE THE PROS & CONS OF BANKRUPTCY

Bankruptcy can offer financial relief to those dealing with unmanageable debt, but like any major financial decision, there are advantages and disadvantages to consider before proceeding. It's necessary to weigh both the potential benefits and drawbacks of bankruptcy carefully before deciding if it's the right choice for your situation.

PROS OF BANKRUPTCY

Bankruptcy can provide a much-needed relief for those struggling with overwhelming debt. Here are some of the benefits of filing for bankruptcy:

1. **Protection from Creditor Harassment:** As soon as a bankruptcy petition is filed, an automatic stay is put in place to stop creditors from collecting debts or taking any actions against the debtor's assets.

2. **Discharge of Debt:** Bankruptcy allows for the discharge of unsecured debts such as medical bills, credit card balances, and personal loans, giving the debtor a fresh start with a clean slate.
3. **Asset Protection:** Depending on the type of bankruptcy filed, certain assets may be protected from creditors, providing a sense of stability and security for the debtor.
4. **Fresh Start:** Bankruptcy provides a chance for a fresh start, by wiping out or restructuring the debt in a manageable way.

Bankruptcy is a formal process that is governed by federal law and overseen by the bankruptcy court, providing a structured and predictable process for the debtor.

However, bankruptcy is not always the best solution and it may not be the right choice for everyone. It's a very good idea to consult with a bankruptcy attorney to determine if bankruptcy is the best option for the debtor's specific situation, and which type of bankruptcy will provide the most benefits.

CONS OF BANKRUPTCY

Bankruptcy is a complex decision that should be carefully considered. While it can provide relief from overwhelming debt, there are also some significant downsides to consider. Here are some of the main disadvantages of bankruptcy:

1. **Credit Impact:** One of the most significant impacts of bankruptcy is its effect on the debtor's credit score. Bankruptcy can make it harder for the debtor to get approved for loans or credit cards in the future and can remain on their credit report for up to 10 years.

2. **Loss of Assets:** Depending on the type of bankruptcy, certain assets may be liquidated or sold in order to pay off creditors. This can cause a loss of property or other assets that the debtor values.

3. **Income Restrictions:** The debtor may not qualify for certain types of bankruptcy due to their income level. For example, Chapter 7 bankruptcy has a means test to determine if the debtor's income is above a certain threshold, and if so, the debtor may not qualify for this type of bankruptcy.

4. **Long-term Impact:** Bankruptcy can have long-term consequences, both financially and emotionally. The debtor may struggle to get approved for credit for several years after the bankruptcy and may have a harder time rebuilding their credit.

5. **Legal Fees:** Bankruptcy can be a costly process, as it often involves hiring a bankruptcy attorney and court filing fees. Additionally, the debtor may have to pay for credit counseling and debtor education as part of the process.

The best way to proceed is to carefully weigh the pros and cons of bankruptcy and consult with a bankruptcy attorney to determine if it's the right option and which type of bankruptcy will be most beneficial for the debtor's specific situation.

Before I conclude the information on bankruptcy, let me share a story with you. Once upon a time, there was a farmer named Jack who faced financial struggles due to a series of bad harvests, increasing expenses, and accumulating debts. His creditors were hounding him for payments, and he was unable to keep up with his bills. In search of assistance, he approached a bankruptcy attorney who informed him about the different types of bankruptcy. After thorough consideration, Jack opted for Chapter 7 bankruptcy, which would involve the liquidation of his non-exempt assets, and the proceeds would be used to pay off his creditors, while some of his debts may be exempt from liquidation and would be discharged.

Jack learned that his mortgage, car loan, and essential farming tools and equipment would be exempt from liquidation. This realization was a relief for Jack, and he understood that bankruptcy was his best option to protect his valued assets and begin anew. Jack filed for Chapter 7 bankruptcy, which allowed him to discharge his unsecured debts such as medical bills and credit card balances, and he was able to maintain his home, car, and tools. With a renewed sense of financial stability, Jack could move forward from his challenging situation.

In closing, the information provided above is for educational purposes only and is not intended to be legal advice. The decision to file for bankruptcy is a personal one and should be made after careful consideration and consultation with a qualified bankruptcy attorney. The author does not endorse or oppose bankruptcy as a financial solution, and encourages individuals to weigh their options carefully and make the decision that is best for them and their families.

DISCLAIMER:

The credit repair tools described in this book are based on extensive research and the experience of professional credit repair specialists. However, it's important to note that each individual's credit situation is unique and results may vary. The author of this book is not responsible for any negative consequences that may arise from implementing these methods. Readers are encouraged to conduct thorough research and seek advice from a financial expert before making any significant changes to their credit.

I would like to provide an additional disclaimer that the information presented in this book is for educational purposes only and should not be taken as legal or financial advice. The author is not responsible for any actions taken by readers based on the information in this book. It is important for readers to do their own due diligence and consult with a qualified professional before making any financial or legal decisions. The author makes no representations or warranties of any kind, express or implied, about the completeness, accuracy, reliability, suitability or availability with respect to the information contained in this book. Any reliance you place on such information is therefore strictly at your own risk.

CONTACT INFORMATION

We'd love to hear from you! If you have any questions, comments, or feedback about the book or our merchandising, please don't hesitate to contact us. You can reach us by email at AtlasPressAd@gmail.com or Info@AtlasPressLLC.com. We appreciate your support and look forward to connecting with you!

I am so grateful for your support in reading my book. If you found value in its content and would like to support my continued writing endeavors, please consider making a small donation. My aim is to keep producing content that motivates and uplifts people while also providing for my family. Your donation will aid me in achieving these goals. You can reach us by email at

AtlasPressAd@gmail.com or Info@AtlasPressLLC.com.

Thank you for your generosity and belief in my work.

We eagerly await your success stories and insights about this book. Please feel free to send your emails about your credit repair experiences. You can also reach out to us for any contributions to help the write.

Atlas Press Publishing, LLC

www.ingramcontent.com/pod-product-compliance
Lightning Source LLC
LaVergne TN
LVHW022049200926
848481LV00003B/840

* 9 7 9 8 2 2 3 5 8 4 5 6 8 *